Legends *of* Animation

John
Lasseter

Legends of Animation

Tex Avery:
Hollywood's Master of Screwball Cartoons

Walt Disney:
The Mouse that Roared

Matt Groening:
From Spitballs to Springfield

William Hanna and Joseph Barbera:
The Sultans of Saturday Morning

Walter Lantz:
Made Famous by a Woodpecker

John Lasseter:
The Whiz Who Made Pixar King

Hayao Miyazaki:
Japan's Premier Anime Storyteller

Genndy Tartakovsky:
From Russia to Coming-of-Age Animator

Legends of Animation

John Lasseter

The Whiz Who Made Pixar King

Jeff Lenburg

CHELSEA HOUSE
An Infobase Learning Company

John Lasseter: The Whiz Who Made Pixar King
Copyright © 2012 by Jeff Lenburg

All rights reserved. No part of this book may be reproduced or utilized in any form or by any means, electronic or mechanical, including photocopying, recording, or by any information storage or retrieval systems, without permission in writing from the publisher. For information contact:

Chelsea House
An Infobase Learning Company
132 West 31st Street
New York NY 10001

T 28728

Library of Congress Cataloging-in-Publication Data
Lenburg, Jeff.
   John Lasseter : the whiz who made Pixar king / Jeff Lenburg.
        p. cm.
   Includes bibliographical references and index.
   ISBN-13: 978-1-60413-840-5 (hardcover : alk. paper)
   ISBN-10: 1-60413-840-8 (hardcover : alk. paper) 1. Lasseter, John—Juvenile literature. 2. Motion picture producers and directors—United States—Biography—Juvenile literature. 3. Animators—United States—Biography—Juvenile literature. 4. Pixar (Firm)—Juvenile literature. I. Title.
   PN1998.3.L3925L46 2011
   791.4302'33092—dc23
   [B]   2011031080

Chelsea House books are available at special discounts when purchased in bulk quantities for businesses, associations, institutions, or sales promotions. Please call our Special Sales Department in New York at (212) 967-8800 or (800) 322-8755.

You can find Chelsea House on the World Wide Web at
http://www.infobaselearning.com

Text design by Kerry Casey
Cover design by Takeshi Takahashi
Composition by EJB Publishing Services
Cover printed by IBT Global, Troy, N.Y.
Book printed and bound by IBT Global, Troy, N.Y.
Date printed: December 2011

Printed in the United States of America

10 9 8 7 6 5 4 3 2 1

This book is printed on acid-free paper.

All links and Web addresses were checked and verified to be correct at the time of publication. Because of the dynamic nature of the Web, some addresses and links may have changed since publication and may no longer be valid.

To Larry and Sandy Lukehart,
for all the love and laughter

CONTENTS

Acknowledgments		9
1	Uncovering His Artistic Passion	11
2	Working at the House that Walt Built	23
3	Taking a Creative Leap	34
4	Championing Computer Animation Byte by Byte	45
5	Toying His Way to Infinity and Beyond!	68
6	Living in a Pixar World	89
7	Restoring the Magic of Disney	104
Selected Resources		124
Selected Bibliography		126
Index		130
About the Author		136

ACKNOWLEDGMENTS

This book would not have been possible without the contributions of many individuals and organizations that provided specific details, insights, and information helpful to the biographer in writing this illuminating volume on the life and career of this icon of animation.

In particular, my thanks to Ars Electronica; Associated Press; CalArts; the Margaret Herrick Library of the Academy of Motion Picture Arts and Sciences; Arizona State University Fletcher Library at the West Campus; Sandy Lukeheart, Fullerton College Library; Pixar Animation Studios; Reuters; the Walt Disney Archive; the Walt Disney Company; and others for kindly giving of their time and material, including articles, books, histories, transcripts, photographs, and other documents vital to the success of this project.

My indebtedness goes to many published sources as well, including the *American Cinematographer*, *Contra Costa Times*, the *Daily News* of Los Angeles, *Entertainment Weekly*, the *Los Angeles Times*, the *New York Times*, *Newsweek*, the *Press Democrat*, the *San Francisco Chronicle*, *San Jose Mercury News*, *Variety*, and countless others that were invaluable in researching and writing this biography.

Finally, thanks to John Lasseter, for your positive influence on audiences of all ages and generations of animators with characters and movies with heart, inventiveness, and high morals, and for unlocking the creative spirit and unlimited potential within each of us.

1

Uncovering His Artistic Passion

Although he never sought to become famous or a household name, his childlike charm, ingenuity, vision, and imagination have brought him the kind of unparalleled worldwide success he never dreamed possible. Since the early 1980s, he has perfected, along with his creative partners under the Pixar banner, three-dimensional computer animation technology that has spawned enormously successful Academy Award-winning shorts and blockbuster movies such as *Toy Story*, *A Bug's Life*, *Toy Story 2*, *Cars*, and *Toy Story 3*. He has created stories and characters with true emotion that have won over audiences and critics alike. Called by many a latter-day Walt Disney, the man behind all of this is none other than John Lasseter.

For John, success did not come immediately, though it appeared early on that he was one of kind. Born unexpectedly in Hollywood, California, on January 12, 1957, when his parents were expecting only the birth of a single child, a daughter, and not paternal twins, he was the so-called "bonus baby" of the family. His sister Johanna preceded him in birth by six minutes and he became the youngest of three children after their oldest brother, Jim. John grew up in Whittier, California, a suburb of Los Angeles, and former President Richard M. Nixon's birthplace. There, his father, Paul Eual Lasseter, worked as a parts manager at the local Chevrolet car dealership and his mother, Jewell Mae, was an art teacher at Bell Gardens Senior High School.

Growing up, John learned to draw and take apart cars. He loved doing both. "Scratch one vein, and it's Disney blood," he later said. "Scratch a second, and it's motor oil."

From an early age, Jewell nurtured John's artistic passions. She brought home paint and paper to encourage his burgeoning drawing skills. As he recalled, "She never formally taught us, but she always surrounded us with art supplies and showed us how to do different little projects—plaster casts, carvings, things like that."

Interestingly, the Lasseter's three children all pursued careers that tapped into their creativity. Johanna later worked as a professional baker of elaborate wedding cakes, while Jim went on to become an accomplished interior designer.

At age five, John's crayon drawing of the Headless Horseman from the classic Washington Irving tale won first place—and a cash prize of $15—from the Model Grocery Market in Whittier, which sponsored the contest. Whether at home or in church, it seemed he was always drawing. During their weekly Sunday worships, Jewell always had pads of paper handy to keep her three children occupied if they began to squirm. Usually that was right after they sat down, so she immediately handed them the paper. John quietly sat in his place and drew the entire time. "I even did flip books in the corner of the songbooks," he later said.

John was like most kids in that on school days his parents had a hard time rustling him out of bed. He was a remarkable daydreamer whose drawings became an extension of his flights of fantasy. He often fantasized in his drawings of tree houses, underground tunnels, secret caves, and flying ships and a group of young adventurers. Sometimes his daydreams extended into the classroom. His teachers contacted his parents "more than once" about his need to pay better attention in class. Even then, considered "the artist of the class," he could not help himself. His mind would be flooded by ideas and stories that he would draw and write down, often losing track of time and becoming lost in his creative world.

Typical of his generation, John loved collecting toys as a kid. His favorites were his Mattel Hot Wheels cars, his G.I. Joe soldiers, and a Casper the Friendly Ghost doll with a pull string on his back that made him talk. John was also a voracious fan of comic strips, particularly Charles M. Schulz's *Peanuts* and Hank Ketchum's *Dennis the Menace*. But his love of comic strips paled to his passion for animated cartoons. As he once stated, "I loved cartoons more than anything else." He was obsessed with cartoons by Warner Bros. cartoon legend Chuck Jones and would race home after school to watch reruns of them on television. On Saturday mornings he would get up at exactly 6:30 and lie on his bed and enjoy a bowl of Kellogg's Sugar Frosted Flakes, a mere six inches from the television set in his bedroom, waiting for the first cartoon to come on. Then he watched them straight through until the last cartoon program ended right before the popular celebrity game show *Bowling for Dollars*.

As he told Jonathan Ross for *Guardian Online*: "Back in the day when I was a little guy there was no home video, or 24-hour cable channels of animation. Animation was on Saturday morning and after school—basically that was it. So when *Bugs Bunny* came on, I was in front of the TV. I just adored it."

Even later after entering high school—when it was, as he called it, "uncool" to like cartoons and toys ("I still had my G.I. Joes and my Hot Wheels")—and he made the school's water polo team, John quietly hurried home after practice to watch cartoons. Lying on his belly on the rust-colored shag carpet of the family's den, he enjoyed the antics of Bugs Bunny, Road Runner and Coyote, and others shown on KTTV channel 11 at 4:30 P.M. "There was no recording it," he recalled. "If you missed it, you missed it."

John was a huge fan of animated films by Walt Disney. His favorite movie while growing up was *Dumbo*, which he called "a perfect movie." As he commented, "It's just 60 minutes long; as a story, it's really tight, and it's incredibly emotional, especially for parents." The most emotional scene in his opinion was the one where Timothy Mouse takes Dumbo to see his mother, a scene backed by the song "Baby Mine." His mother, deemed "a mad elephant," is locked away, and they cannot see each other but only touch trunks. John also found *Dumbo* "the most cartoony" of all the Disney films, in his view.

Little did John realize that someday he would become a major force in the animation business himself. But the seed was being planted for greater things to come.

The turning point for John's interest in animation happened in ninth grade as a freshman at Whittier High School. He was perusing the art section of his school's library, looking for a book to write a report on for class and stumbled across a beat-up copy of *The Art of Animation*, an illustrated history of Disney Studios, by longtime Associated Press entertainment writer Bob Thomas. After reading the book, his immediate reaction was, "Wait a minute, people do this for a living?"

John has called this one of the key moments of his life that guided him on the path he followed. "Finding that book was one of them. I read it from cover to cover," he said. It was right at the point in time that he decided animation was what he wanted to do for a living.

Not long after this eye-opening experience, John went to see a 49-cent showing of Walt Disney's animated feature *The Sword in the Stone*, at the art deco-styled Wardman Theatre downtown. His mother had dropped him off and picked him up, and he experienced an epiphany afterward, telling her during the drive back home, "I'm going to work for Walt Disney." She was nothing but encouraging. "That's a great goal to have," she told him. John has admitted in interviews that he had no idea at the time how rare that kind of support from a parent was, but his mother always felt strongly that pursuing the arts was "a noble profession."

Studying art as a teenager, John began perfecting his talent by doing traditional hand-drawn animation before later pioneering computer animation. With his goal in plain sight, he began writing to Walt Disney Studios about his desire to become an animator. Ultimately he corresponded with Ed Hansen, the manager of Disney's animation department. His letters to Hansen paid off when he invited John for a tour of the studio. When John visited, Hansen encouraged him to lay a strong foundation for his career in college: Get an art education and

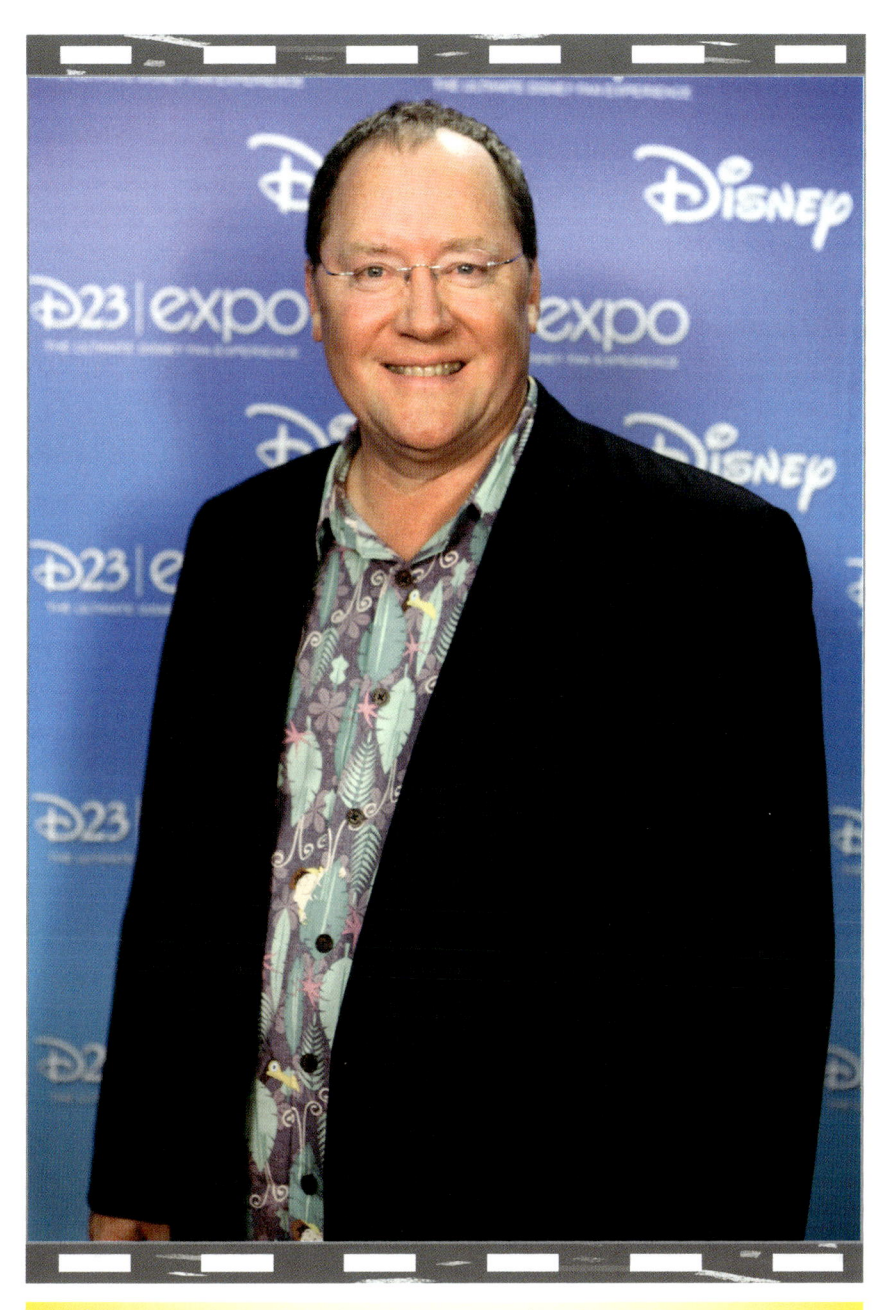

Lasseter, as he looks today, characteristically wearing a Hawaiian shirt to round out his wardrobe.

learn the basics of figure drawing, design, color, and they would teach him animation.

SEEKING HIS CARTOON DREAMS

John was willing and ready to do whatever it took as his mind was made up. There was not anything he would love to do more than to work as an animator. Opportunity knocked when he least expected it. During the start of his senior year in high school in 1974, he was surprised by what he found after coming home from school one day. Waiting for him was a letter from Walt Disney Studios announcing the formation of a new character animation program at California Institute of the Arts (CalArts), the art school Walt Disney had founded that had become a major talent pool for his Burbank studio, to start the following year.

John shook with excitement as he read every word of the letter. This was another one of those key moments in his life. His destiny was right in front of him. He immediately acted by submitting his portfolio to be considered for the program and was the second applicant accepted. Legendary Disney animator/director Jack Hannah, who headed the program and was best known for directing many Oscar-winning *Donald Duck* cartoons, invited John to become his student assistant for the summer and help prepare materials for the fall start-up of the program.

John naturally accepted and started in his new position after graduating from Whittier High. His job involved choosing the best material from the studio's archive—animation drawings, backgrounds, and layouts from Disney movies—and photocopying them for students to use for study purposes. In his newly created position he had unfettered access to most of the studio and consequently met and struck up friendships with several other young and up-and-coming artists in the studio's animation training program, among them a young animator by the name of Glen Keane.

Recalling his friendship with the young aspiring animator, Keane once related: "Lasseter then wasn't any different than he is now. He is like a duck in water when he was dealing with animation—completely comfortable. This was his element; he knew everything about it."

Working that summer as Hannah's assistant was a remarkable experience for John and was a precursor of greater things to come for him. That fall, he began his postsecondary education at Malibu's prestigious Pepperdine University (his parents' alma mater) before deciding to really follow his passion and enroll in courses at CalArts. He immediately recognized after being in the program a short time how special it was. He was taught by three of Walt Disney's surviving "Nine Old Men" responsible for creating the studio's classic animated films: Eric Larson, Frank Thomas, and Ollie Johnston, and other longtime Disney artists from Hollywood's golden age of animation: director Jack Hannah; animator and director Thornton "T." Hee; art director and layout artist Kendall O'Connor; and art director and storyboard artist Elmer Plummer. He was also fortunate to be instructed in design by veteran instructor Bill Moore, previously associated with CalArts's predecessor, the Chouinard Art Institute.

John thrived at CalArts in that first class in 1975. He was surrounded by many equally talented, budding artists whose passion for animation was equal to his own. His classmates in the program included Brad Bird, who later made a mark for himself as the director of Warner Bros.'s *The Iron Giant* and Pixar's *The Incredibles*; Chris Buck, who eventually codirected Disney's animated film *Tarzan*; Tim Burton, who used his work in animation as a platform and an integral part of his later films, such as *Batman* and *The Nightmare Before Christmas*; and John Musker, who later codirected such Disney blockbuster features as *The Little Mermaid*, *Aladdin*, and *Hercules*.

For John and his comrades in the arts, their whole focus as students was studying filmmaking, character development, and storytelling. As a result, they lived and breathed animation day and night. "There was this amazing camaraderie," John recalled.

"Everyone was on fire about animation, and we didn't want to leave at the end of the day," Bird told author-filmmaker Leslie Iwerks.

At night after classes, 10 classmates, including John, would go out to dinner and check out old 16 mm prints of Disney classic features like

Dumbo and watch them on school projectors afterward, studying them closely and analyzing them one frame at a time. "We wore out those prints analyzing them," John recalled. He has said they learned nearly as much from each other as they did from their instructors because "we were all so into it, and spent so much time together."

John fed off the collaborative spirit of the program and found it entirely inspiring. It was that kind of collaborative environment and openness he would re-create years later at Pixar. Each man worked extremely hard at their craft but at the same time had a lot of fun— they would laugh, goof off, and work together while giving each other important feedback on each other's work.

In late May 1977, another defining moment strongly impacted John's life. He and several classmates went on opening weekend in a packed house to Mann's Chinese Theatre in Hollywood to watch one of the most anticipated science-fiction movies of the summer: *Star Wars*. It exceeded his wildest expectations. The futuristic fantasy film's incredible special effects astounded him. In John's words, it had "the goods." As he added, "No one had ever seen anything like it before. The crowd just went nuts. You've never seen an audience as pumped to see a movie as that. You were having so much fun and were so into this film, you were just shaking by the end of it."

As he looked around and saw in the audience such a great cross-section of kids, adults, teenagers, and college students, John experienced yet another epiphany. He thought to himself, "Animation can do this [too]."

John left the theater that day inspired. While other friends abandoned animation and went into doing special effectives for live-action movies, the experience reaffirmed his commitment to his chosen medium. "It made me rededicate myself to animation. I believed that animation could be entertaining on that level," he said. "That it could be that big. I wanted to show it was possible to make something that could reach everyone, not just kids."

Out of school for the summer, John landed a job at Disneyland, Walt Disney's sprawling amusement park and "Happiest Place on Earth" in Anaheim, California, an hour east of Los Angeles. His first

Uncovering His Artistic Passion 19

Lasseter in the early days of his career. Courtesy: ARS Electronica

job was as a sweeper in Tomorrowland. While others considered his kind of work menial, he saw things differently. He enjoyed being out among the guests and summer crowds—who turned out in mass for the opening of the newest attraction, Space Mountain—and he found the whole experience exciting.

Months later John transferred to a new job: as a ride operator for the Jungle Cruise. He was responsible for working as the river cruise guide and being part of the whole show by talking through a loudspeaker to guests on their swampy adventure. He was nervous his first day as he had trouble remembering lines but once the ride started everything "clicked" and he started having fun with it, doing voices and more. By the time the ride was over, people clapped appreciatively of his efforts.

In performing the same material hundreds of times, John learned much on the job that he could apply to animation. One thing he learned was the importance of impeccable comic timing and pacing and delivery to achieve the best end result. Likewise he gained a better understanding of how to read an audience, "tweak" his material when something was not working, and make the relationship between the different parts work. As he noted in the illustrated history *To Infinity and Beyond!*, "In animation, you work on your material for such a long time. You come to know it inside out. By the time you're done making the movie, you will have seen that joke, that line, that drawing, a thousand times, and it will no longer be funny. And a lot of times people will say, 'it's not funny anymore, let's try to make it funny,' and in trying to 'fix' it, they break it. So I always tell people never to forget the first time something made you laugh."

After two years of a classic art education at CalArts, during his last years in the program John's education was a mix of studio classes and producing short films. In his junior year he produced his first project, *Lady and the Lamp*. This black-and-white film, animated entirely in pencil, illustrates the chaos that results in a lamp store where all the lamps come alive and one little lamp gets knocked off a shelf and breaks its light bulb and goes blind. Fumbling his way through the shop, he tries to find another light bulb and ends up screwing in a gin bottle and gets drunk, destroying the store in the process. The film was the first and only one of John's early cartoon shorts to use dialogue, with the shopkeeper as the only character that talks. The short would become an important first step in his fledgling career, showcasing his inherent ability to bring to life inanimate objects that were sympathetic and entertaining, becoming a trademark of his work. Of the lamp gone wild, he later said, "I wanted to get the sense that he was a character without doing the typical thing of sticking a face on an inanimate object. And I think I succeeded."

One of his CalArts instructors, T. Hee, who was also a governor of the Academy of Motion Picture Arts and Sciences, recommended that John submit his film for consideration of the Student Academy Award. He complied and, much to his surprise, he won the award in 1979 for animation.

The following year, with every CalArts student producing their films with dialogue, John decided to do his next project without it and "just let the film play by itself." As a result, he produced and directed his second film about things that go "bump" in the night, *Nitemare*, which some claim appears to borrow from Mercer Mayer's warm, funny illustrated 1968 children's book, *There's a Nightmare in My Closet*. The three-minute film, about a boy who learns to relate to monsters that visit his bedroom right after the lights go out, was challenging to do without dialogue but won John more kudos, including his second Student Academy Award in as many years at the Academy's Seventh Annual Student Film Awards held at the Samuel Goldwyn Theater in Beverly Hills.

A common thread in his work that began back then was his penchant for "animating the inanimate," something John would take to new heights in the future. To make his work more interesting, however, he enjoyed taking on new challenges. As he said later, reflecting on his earlier accomplishments, "I love being challenged with things. In almost every film I made, there's some sort of challenge I placed on myself. The *Lady and the Lamp* is the story of a lamp shop where the lamps are alive, but there's no face on the main character, because he breaks his light bulb and goes looking for another light bulb. So to get across a personality with no face was a challenge. The following year in *Nitemare*, the big challenge for me was the fact that there was no dialogue at all, to tell the story visually without any dialogue. I find it real interesting. It's a challenge to be able to take something like a lamp that looks like a lamp and give it a personality. Also the audience finds a lot of humor in that these are just lamps, acting human."

In 1979, John graduated from CalArts with a Bachelor of Fine Arts in Film, preparing him to work in the job of his dreams—as an animator—and at the place where classic animation was born: Walt Disney Studios.

2

Working at the House that Walt Built

Having apprenticed at Walt Disney Studios the past two summers before graduating, John was ready for more. He was anxious to launch his animation career and nothing was going to get in the way.

John's first choice was to become an animator at Walt Disney Studios. The studio hired him immediately after he graduated to work as an animator in its feature animation department in the animation building at Mickey Avenue and Dopey Drive on the Disney lot. He can thank two coinciding events for his arrival. The first happened the week before he began work. Frustrated by the quality and artistic timidity of the studio's films, a dozen animators quit along with Don Bluth, the leader of this faction, to form their own studio with Bluth, thus creating openings that had to be filled. The second one happened on the night John graduated. During the graduation ceremony Bob Fitzpatrick, then president of CalArts, told Ron Miller, then the head of Walt Disney Studios, that "John Lasseter is something very special and you better let him have something to do there, because he wants it and [otherwise] maybe he won't stay."

John was too happy to be working at Walt Disney Studios to think much about the circumstances that led to his hiring, but grateful for the opportunity, nonetheless. It meant he and his fellow hired graduates—

Brad Bird, Tim Burton, Dan Haskett, Glen Keane, Bill Kroyer, John Musker, Jerry Rees, and Henry Selick—would be able to work with five of Walt's elite class of animators, or "Nine Old Men," and true legends in the business: Ollie Johnston, Marc Davis, Eric Larson, Woolie Reitherman, and Frank Thomas. They were given the task of mentoring the studio's young animators.

John felt extremely fortunate to work with Thomas and Johnston, whose classic feature animation, in his words, "had so much heart." He equated them to actors who had created many milestone moments on film using two critical elements at the core of their foundation: story and character. On some afternoons he spent hours in the offices of both studio legends, whose door was always open to young animators who worked under their tutelage. John often shared with them scenes he had animated. They freely gave him notes of critical feedback and talked to him about his work. "They were starting to work on *The Illusion of Life* [a book they cowrote] at the time," John later stated, "and so much of what would later go into that book was stuff I was able to get firsthand from them. It was unbelievable."

Even then, despite their generational differences, younger animators like John immediately bonded with these masters of their craft. These men had been carrying the torch for quality animation for many years and were ready to pass it on to their believers like they were "apostles."

The glory days of Disney feature animation, however, had largely passed. The studio's zenith was between the mid-'30s and '50s during which time Walt Disney had claimed numerous landmark achievements to his credit and had acquired a reputation for innovation and quality in his work. Through his leadership, he left his personal stamp on every production. He was obsessed with making every project better and experimenting with new techniques that resulted in significant advances in animation—from introducing the idea of "personality animation," which is making characters more realistic and lifelike, to producing countless classic theatrical shorts and features that reached new plateaus, starting with the studio's first foray into feature-length animation—and the first full-length color feature ever made—*Snow

White and the Seven Dwarfs (1937). In the '60s and '70s, though, outside of Walt's longtime collaborator Ub Iwerks inventing the technique of Xerography—where drawings were photocopied directly to cels—for 1961's *One Hundred and One Dalmatians*, the technical flourishes and innovations that had become the hallmark of Walt's cartoon kingdom remained stuck in neutral. Without his unique vision and leadership since his death in 1966, the studio's animated features, though beautifully hand-drawn, inked, and painted with some brilliant moments, were not up to the same standards as Walt's. As many of his stalwart animators began to retire or die, only a few were left to carry the torch by

The kid-at-heart Lasseter in his office surrounded by his collection of collectible toys that keep him grounded. *Photo: Mel Melcon/Los Angeles Times.* © *Los Angeles Times*

the time John had joined Disney to guide the studio's new generation of artists entering the business. They did so without the kind of creative continuity that had been there in the past.

TROUBLING TIMES

While Disney's first new crop of animators from CalArts had real potential yet to be realized, the atmosphere they created for their budding artists was nothing like what Walt had inspired or John had imagined. It was rigid, restrictive, stifling, and hardly magical. Run by lesser artists and business people who rose to their positions through attrition, the studio's creative leadership was largely dispassionate about what the new, young, excited recruits had to offer, and as John recalled "didn't know how to handle us and worked really hard to keep us under control." Coming from CalArts, John was used to a system where his colleagues were impassioned and enthusiastic, supportive and critical of each other's work, and drew ideas from each other. At Disney, such a collegial environment was all but nonexistent.

"It was stifling," John recalled. "They really went to great effort to squish the young talent. The creative leadership at the time was these guys who were kind of second-tier animators. I didn't want control, power—that's what they were into. I just wanted to make the movies better. The famous saying back then was, 'What would Walt do?' Walt died in 1966! The studio had been hermetically sealed."

John and his up-and-coming colleagues wanted to do *Star Wars*-level films with animation. But the studio's creative brain trust wanted to keep on the same creative path of repeating itself without adding any news ideas or innovations. That direction did not include the kind of spark of creativity for blending filmmaking with new cutting-edge technology that John had in mind. In John's opinion the studio had reached its plateau with the original *One Hundred and One Dalmatians* and had not taken any steps beyond, using old technology and old methods of making animated movies.

For John the luster of working at Disney wore off after he encountered resistance to his ideas while he and fellow animator Glen Keane were animating the studio's latest feature *The Fox and the Hound*. He and Keane suggested to those in charge some changes to add more tension and excitement to the film's finale, which later wound up in the movie though they were at first turned down. One of them told John, "Look, we don't want to hear your ideas; just do what you're told. There are plenty of guys who'd be happy to take your place."

Another saw John's suggestions more as a threat than a help. Instead of embracing his ideas, he gave him a blistering undressing. "So you want to be creatively in charge here? I'll tell you how to be in charge," he ranted. "You sit down and do in-betweens for 20 years, *then* you can be in charge."

John found this all too hard to fathom. This was the same studio whose work he had idolized as a kid and that had become known for breakthrough innovations in animation and techniques of filmmaking throughout its history. He was so disgusted afterward that he left Disney, the studio of his dreams, to work for London-based animator Richard Williams's animation studio. Williams was best known to audiences then for producing animated title openings for two *Pink Panther* movies and for his Academy Award-winning version of *A Christmas Carol*. Not much happier in his new surroundings, John returned to Disney within a year.

John still had a strong desire bubbling under the surface to improve his work and seek new technologies if necessary to achieve his goal more effectively. He kept thinking to himself, "What's going to be the new thing that takes animation to the next level?" The idea was right before him—literally.

While working on *The Fox and the Hound*, John discovered a stash of videotapes from one of the new computer graphics conferences of that time. They illustrated the beginnings of computer animation, like floating spheres and such, indoctrinating him into the possibilities of how this technology could be used in films. That would become a reference point for him in the future. Even though computer graphics was still in its infancy and its primary application had thus far been in television commercials, John never gave up his pursuit of using this technology more broadly in films.

After completing his work on *The Fox and the Hound*, released to theaters in 1981, John began to work in the studio's story department on a number of projects that did not "get off the ground," and then as an animator on a new featurette, *Mickey's Christmas Carol*, later broadcast on television as an animated special. While he was assigned that project, however, something truly innovative was in the works, something so un-Disney-like that it was on the cutting edge of technology. It was so groundbreaking that it created a tremendous buzz of excitement and anticipation not seen in years. The project was *TRON*.

The first film to make computer graphics an integral part of it, *TRON* represented new territory for Disney, creating a true three-dimensional world combining live action and computer animation. Requiring nearly 30 minutes of film-quality computer graphics was a daunting task, given the state of computer graphics technology at the time. Three different companies were chosen to produce the effects—MAGI/Synthavision of Elmsford, New York; Digital Effects of New York; and III (Triple-I) of Los Angeles. Meanwhile John's friends and fellow animators Bill Kroyer and Jerry Rees were holed up in a trailer on the Disney back lot, busy storyboarding and choreographing the computer graphics for the futuristic, state-of-the-art feature. One day they invited John to see what would become one of the film's "iconic" scenes of two MAGI/Synthavision-created lightcycles streaking across a virtual landscape. Threading the film made with a computer through an old 1930s Moviola, John was immediately awestruck by what flickered in front of him on the tiny glass screen as Bill and Jerry looked on. "I was immediately blown away by the potential of the images," he recalled.

John was impressed by how the visual effects in Kroyer's and Rees's segments using computer graphics had produced "more dimensionality into animation backgrounds" than by hand-drawn animation. As a result, it did not take him long to see the tremendous effect this technology would have on animation, and how computers could be used to produce movies with three-dimensional backgrounds combined with traditionally animated characters. This could add greater and more visually stunning depth not possible with a multiplane camera (a technique invented in the 1930s that gave animated cartoons the illusion of three-dimension) and never attempted before. As John added, "I saw the dailies for it, although I had always worked in traditional cel animation, whole new worlds opened up for me when I saw the computer-animated visual effects they used. I got real excited about computer graphics."

TRYING SOMETHING NEW

One brilliant animator shared his excitement of blazing a new path in animation: Glen Keane. Finding the whole idea of working with a new dimension irresistible, they forged ahead to immediately realize the promise of combining computer animation with live action to achieve greater three-dimensionality on film. When they got together, their imaginations ran wild and they started to believe, "Why can't we do that?" They settled on a "cool" idea they had hatched: animating traditional hand-drawn Disney-like characters moving against a computer-animated dimensional background as in *TRON*.

John took his idea of applying *TRON*-type computer graphics with traditional animation to Disney's head of animation, who immediately said, "No, we can't do that."

So John went around him. He met with Tom Wilhite, then head of production of Walt Disney Studios and who supervised production of *TRON*, about producing a 30-second test using their innovative concept. Wilhite happened to have a development arrangement with popular children's book author Maurice Sendak and agreed to them adapting the characters, Max and his dog, from his widely successful book, *Where the Wild Things Are*, for their test film.

Teaming up with Keane, John designed and directed one of the first computer-generated imagery (CGI) projects ever conceived. Working together was a good fit for their talents: John's expressive, computer-oriented animation and technical command of the advancing medium and Keane's solid characterizations and fast, fluid drawing style. John worked alongside MAGI/Synthavision's Chris Wedge, who later went on to direct Blue Sky Studio's smash hit feature *Ice Age*, modeling the environment and blocking the scenes to aid Keane in animating the characters. Their unfinished film demonstrated how hand-drawn animation could be successfully combined with computerized camera movements and environments. The techniques they used were essentially the same as those used nine years later to create the scene of the Beast dancing with his Belle in a virtual ballroom in Disney's *Beauty and the Beast*, when such technology had come of age.

Before completing their *Wild Things* test film to show to studio executives, the unimaginable happened: an advanced screening of *TRON* produced a "chilly reception," and in July 1982, the studio's new partially computer-animated fantasy-adventure opened in theaters mostly to lukewarm reviews. Disney sunk around $20 million into the cyber-adventure and, though the computer-generated imagery was technologically dazzling, the underlying story was unappealing. The film bombed at the box office. Iconic studio animator Frank Thomas was one of the old guard who saw computer animation as having a future. "Gee, if you can get that much imagination and types of movement in there by a computer, not a pencil," he once said, "you'll be ahead of the game!"

With nearly 95 of the studio's artists apprehensive of this innovative art form, saying, "You'll never get me to do any computer animation," combined with Disney's financial losses, the studio's powers-that-be all but killed the idea of doing more productions using this technology that they deemed, as John recalled, "just too expensive." This was not apparent to John until it was too late.

Consequently, John and Keane switched gears. After producing the test film, John suggested they have a story ready so they could show the test and say, "Here, let's make a feature like this with this story." He wanted to develop a feature in the same style as their completed test film. In the interim one of his friends, John Debney, knowing of John's fondness for "animating the inanimate," turned him on to something he felt was the perfect property for what he had in mind: a feature treatment of Thomas Disch's novella, *The Brave Little Toaster*. Still supportive of John and Keane's project, Tom Wilhite optioned the book and John began to develop it with his friends Brian McEntee and Joe Ranft while he and Keane continue working on their *Wild Things* test film. The original plan was to produce a feature of *The Brave Little Toaster* much like the former with hand-animated characters on computer-generated backgrounds. John started scouting companies to find the right one to handle the computer graphics and one of them he visited was Lucasfilm in Northern California.

Meeting with Lucasfilm principals Ed Catmull and Alvy Ray Smith, John wowed them with the screening of his novel use of computer graphics in his and Keane's *Wild Things* test. A computer scientist and pioneer in computer graphics from New York Institute of Technology, Catmull served as vice president of Lucasfilm's Computer Graphics Division launched in 1979. After the stunning special effects achievement of his blockbuster movie, *Star Wars*, famed filmmaker George Lucas persuaded Catmull and his colleague Smith to head the new division within Lucasfilm to create computer technology to allow computer-generated effects to be combined with live action for his studio's feature films. Together they recruited a team of outstanding people from the still-young field of computer graphics to develop computer technology, including REYES (Renders Everything You Ever Saw) that would eventually become Pixar's rendering engine, RenderMan, to specifically handle imaging tasks for the motion picture industry. The new unit complemented Lucas's other company, Industrial Light & Magic, whose original purpose was to develop digital sound, a video editing system (dubbed "The Droid Works"), and computer graphics for special effects.

John discussed with them the prospects of having Lucasfilm produce the computer-generated backgrounds for *The Brave Little Toaster*, and they met a second time back at Disney Studios in Burbank. Although he and Catmull developed an immediate rapport, Catmull, unfortunately, passed on the project. He did not believe Lucasfilm's Computer Graphics Division was in the position to contract out its services at that time.

Upon his return, John learned that while forging ahead with Wilhite's blessings that he was to immediately show his test film and present his pitch for *The Brave Little Toaster* to Disney studio head Ron Miller, Walt Disney's son-in-law, and Ed Hansen, the manager of the animation department. He had no idea what he was walking into that day but felt rather uneasy about the whole situation. Much to his surprise, he found his attempts to improve animation in the calcifying company only resulted in animus. "I didn't realize it then, but I was beginning to be perceived as a loose cannon. All I was trying to do was make things greater, but I was beginning to make some enemies," he stated.

When a grim-faced Miller walked in to the room with Hansen at his side, John could tell his pitch was going to be a "hard sell." Nonetheless he enthusiastically ran through the concept for them. As he finished, Miller stood up and asked how much such a production would cost. John stated that it would cost "no more than a regular film." Unimpressed, Miller stood up. He said he did not see the point in making the production with computer animation. He stated, "The only reason to produce this by computer is if it makes it cheaper and faster," and walked out. Consequently, John's idea for a full-fledged, longer experimental film of *The Brave Little Toaster* was shot down.

John was a bit perplexed and nonplussed after the meeting ended. Five minutes later, Hansen called him and asked to see him. When he got to his office, he had no sooner sat down when Hansen said, "Well, John, your project is now complete, so your employment with the Disney Studios is now terminated."

As John recalled, "I couldn't believe it. I had just been fired."

John had tried his best to convince Disney executives of the unlimited potential and possibilities of computer graphics and computer animation. But "to them, animation had become just for kids," he remarked, "which was sad for me."

After John's dismissal that fall, Wilhite arranged to keep him on board in the live-action department until he completed the *Wild Things* test. Believing in his heart he would achieve his life's ambition after becoming an animator for Disney, John found the experience "a crushing disappointment." The dejected animator told colleagues he simply had left on his own accord. "To be fired from the place of my dreams was something I just couldn't admit," he said.

The firing was devastating to John for many other reasons. "When you're young," he added, "your identity is wrapped up in this dream. To have the rug pulled out from under me was so disheartening."

Glum and depressed, John contemplated his future. That November, he attended a computer graphics conference aboard the Queen Mary, a retired ocean liner converted to a museum ship and hotel, in Long Beach, California, where he ran into someone unexpected: Ed Catmull. Catmull, a scheduled speaker at the conference, was glad to see John and immediately asked about the project. John informed him, "It got shelved," and that he had been let go. They exchanged a few more pleasantries and then John went back into the conference.

An hour later as he sat and listened to a "boring speaker" in the Queen Mary's majestic grand ballroom, while thinking about how he could still produce his *Toaster* film, he suddenly heard a whisper in his ear. He looked over his shoulder and standing off to the side of him was Catmull. John immediately got up and walked over to him. He said, "John, I was just talking to Alvy. Since you're not really doing anything, do you want to come up and do a little freelance job? We're thinking about doing something with character animation with the computer."

John was not sure what to think as it all seemed "a little weird to me at the time—I had always thought the computer would be for backgrounds," he said, "and the character animation would be done by hand."

With nothing else going on in his life, he thought, "Yeah, why not?"

In late 1983, John took two more trips, spending an entire week in December, to meet with Catmull at the Lucasfilm Computer Graphics Division to get a better handle on the kind of work he would be doing and a better idea of the ebb and flow of the company. For John, this sudden opportunity was about to take him down a new path, to see where his talent would take him and achieve his desires while ushering in a new age that would forever transform the industry in ways that seemed unimaginable back then even to him.

3

Taking a Creative Leap

In January 1984, with his association with Disney Studios officially ending after completing his *Wild Things* test film, John turned his life around. Accepting Catmull's invitation to join them for a month, he moved to the Bay Area, where he began freelancing full time as what they called an interface designer instead of animator, so that nobody would question his hiring at budget meetings for Lucasfilm. One month evolved into six and John stayed much longer than he had anticipated.

For two years, John had collected the best representative samples of computer-generated images and realized afterward that the people's work he admired the most of all were with Lucasfilm. Instantly floored by the body of their work, after having been there only a short time, he asked Catmull, "How did you get all these people? These guys are the best in the world."

"Well, I try to hire people that are smarter than myself," Catmull said, with a laugh.

John found Catmull's statement rather insightful. It showed how secure he was of himself and of his own ability to hire great people and let them "shine." The atmosphere was completely opposite of Disney, where studio executives, too afraid about the bottom line and insecure about their own futures, tamped down their young, talented, and enthusiastic animators instead of encouraging them and letting them blossom. Instead, partly because of Catmull's science background, he encouraged new ideas. "With science there is this culture of experimentation and most of the time those experiments fail," John later explained. "There's a culture of failure, which is accepted. . . ."

Working in a division that was composed of a small group in the beginning, John became the first traditional animator to do computer animation and blossomed in his new position. Many people around him had Ph.D.s, however, and he was a little intimidated at first in his new surroundings. As he stated, "I knew I was never going to be able to learn how to problem solve like they could. But then I realized they couldn't bring a character to life with personality and emotion through pure movement like I could."

John instead took the collaborative approach, matching his strengths in story and character animation with theirs in programming. From his days at Disney, he understood the importance of character and that, as he put it, "Every moment should create the idea that is generated by that character's own thought process." Impressions forever ingrained in him from his Disney days would become hallmarks of his work. One colleague to play a pivotal role in his success, joining the division in 1980, was the in-house computer whiz William Reeves. Later their pairings would bear fruit and turn the computer graphics industry on its head by their stunning achievements.

Early on, John hooked up with Catmull, a frustrated animator himself, to experiment with new tools for creating computer graphics. Despite his unpleasant departure from Disney, John still envisioned using computers mostly for background animation and hand-drawn animation for animating characters in the films he would produce. Catmull convinced him, however, to animate a complete short by computer. He hired him to design and animate the lead character in a one-minute short, dubbed *My Breakfast with André*, originally as an homage to Louis Malle's popular 1981 art-house feature film, *My Dinner with André*, starring Andre Gregory and Wallace Shawn. John cowrote with Alvy Ray Smith, who also directed, the whimsical 3-D film, which he subsequently renamed *The Adventures of André & Wally B.*

During its development, as Reeves produced computer-generated backgrounds using particle systems, a technique employed to simulate moving objects in computer animation, John created the concept art and design the old-fashioned way by hand-drawing it in pencil. Keeping the computer's limitations in mind, he concocted the film's characters as geometric and sphere-shaped forms based on Catmull's teardrop-shaped design to give them the greater flexibility and exude the right kind of expressiveness for being computer animated. Playing with Catmull's design template, John immediately settled on Wally B. as a "big fat bumblebee with these gigantic water balloon-like feet hanging from him—with no visible legs—and a big stainless-steel stinger."

John viewed his transition from cel to computer animation more like doing stop-motion animation than cel animation. "Computer animation is model (or stop motion) animation with the same kind of control you have in drawn animation," he told *American Cinematographer* in 1989. "It's a combination of the two. . . . Obviously the big difference is that the computer is truly a three-dimensional environment."

In his first computer-animated film, John functioned much like a director or animator does in creating traditional animated films. He would come up with the initial concepts and bounce ideas off his crew. Though most of them had computer backgrounds, as he once noted, over the years they had become "quite savvy" with animation and stories. In most cases they would develop the stories together with John storyboarding the project. As he explained, "From the storyboard we define what needs to be modeled. We generally divide up the modeling task between the crew. I'll do some modeling, and then I'll do all the animation, generally. Some of the other people have started doing a little bit of the animation. I also direct it as far as what it looks like, color decisions, staging it, doing the angles. It's sort of up to me to keep the story line together in my head. And then Bill and Eben [Ostby] usually are the ones who render it, after I'm finished doing the animation."

BREAKING NEW GROUND

The Adventures of André & Willy B. was produced using methods similar to John's later successful Pixar films in three stages. First came building the foundation, or the modeling phase, of a 3-D character starting with a 2-D drawing featuring the dimensions of the character—a description of shapes and joints, lengths and widths, heights and breadths—entered into the computer. Next followed the animation phase—also called the "articulation" of the objects—where the movements of a character or object, where they begin and end and every point between, are programmed. The final stage was rendering, where the tones, the shadows, the surfaces, and lighting of a 2-D and 3-D color character or object are finalized, a slow process that literally takes days and weeks, and is one reason computer animation produced at that time was of shorter length than what is often produced today.

Working with the fastest computers available then, producing the computer imagery at Lucasfilm took hours to generate a single image. The current technology handicapped John's efforts somewhat as he was only able to review different parts of the image individually, sometimes days apart. Nonetheless *The Adventures of André & Wally B.* would become the first to use motion blur in CG animation and complex 3-D backgrounds, along with squash-and-stretch style animation of CG models that until then had been restricted to rigid geometric shapes. The animation was rendered on a Cray X-MP/48 supercomputer and 10 VAX-11/750 super minicomputers from Project Athena, originally a distributed computer system created in the early 1980s for educational use that expanded into the area of computer graphics. Beginning with this film, John also made sound effects a signature element of his films, enlisting Ben Burtt, winner of multiple Oscars for sound for *Star Wars* and *Raiders of the Lost Ark*, to produce the film's unique sound effects.

Much like animators working in other mediums—sand, clay, or cel animation—John quickly learned that he needed to understand what could or could not be done to succeed in his new virtual playground. "I know exactly what areas are very important to me but difficult to do, and those areas are the kinds of places we focus in on," he said. "There are a lot of people who are just letting the computer do the animation. You can just type in 'Character Walk,' and it'll walk someplace. That takes the fun out of it for the animator. So what we've done is always keep the animator in initial control, and then let the computer do some of the more mundane stuff."

Lasseter and technical director Bill Reeves digitize shapes from a three-dimensional model of the Stained Glass Knight character for the movie *Young Sherlock Holmes* (1985). *Courtesy: American Cinematographer*

That said, computer animation was far from perfect and had its share of limitations and stumbling blocks to overcome, much that traditional animation did not have and vice versa. "As soon as I started working with computer animation, I realized that the easiest thing to do in hand-drawn animation are the most difficult to do in computer animation," he told *Animato* magazine. "An example of that is organic shapes like Dopey and all the great animation of the Dwarfs. You see that and it's just so fluid, and yet it seems connected. That's so hard to do with computer animation; it's virtually impossible. It's easy to make a sphere or any object scale in X, Y, or Z, but to make something move around and keep the same volume is so hard."

The Adventures of André & Wally B. originally premiered as a mix of final animation and wire-frame pencil tests at the July 24–26, 1984 SIGGRAPH convention, the world's largest annual computer graphics conference for members of the Association for Computing Machinery's Special Interest Group on Graphics, in Minneapolis. Lucasfilm founder George Lucas flew out to attend the film's conference debut. At that year's show, Lucasfilm also introduced a new computer specifically designed to handle complex tasks of manipulating and assembling picture components into a print-ready image: the Pixar Image Computer, developed by Adam Levinthal, Rodney Stock, and Tom Porter.

Few on hand, however, would remember that *The Adventures of André & Wally B.* was incomplete. The fanciful film, including John's whimsical creations zipping across the screen and entirely unlike flying logos, commercials, and demo reels customarily shown at SIGGRAPH, was truly groundbreaking. Released theatrically on December 18, in its completed form, the full-color, 1-minute and 50-seconds short, a series of comical chases involving the bulbous-nosed André (who resembles a beach ball in tennis shoes) and pesky bee, Wally B., bent on stinging him until he has the last laugh, won over industry people and audiences alike.

The Adventures of André & Willy B. ultimately sparked greater interest in computer animation within the film industry besides taking John to new plateaus in his career. He was careful not to take too much credit for his success, however, citing two iconic animation figures as primary influences who were instrumental in his professional development and growth: Walt Disney, whose films, in his words, were "just brilliant in their staging and characters," and Chuck Jones, because, as a director, he had "the greatest timing." Something else Jones said of how, with really good animation, "you should be able to turn the sound off and still know what's going on" he also took to heart, becoming "the foundation of my stories in a lot of ways."

John also credited Disney animation legends Frank Thomas and Ollie Johnston. As he once recalled, "The reason I like their work so much is that they do such great characters. I love the work of Ward Kimball as well; he's a big influence. But his work and Milt Kahl's work are much more identifiable. You'll look at Milt Kahl's work and say, 'Oh, there's a Milt Kahl scene.' His stuff is *brilliant*, but I think Frank Thomas and Ollie Johnston do work where the character is it, is everything, and their stuff just comes alive."

As for his use of color in his cartoons, he considered Oscar-winning animator-director Norman McLaren and his series of films, *Animation Motion*, "wonderful teaching tools."

Though he enjoyed the idyllic work environment at Lucasfilm, after he returned to Los Angeles from SIGGRAPH, he accepted an offer too tempting to pass up. Tom Wilhite had left Disney and was planning to produce *The Brave Little Toaster* as an independent feature and wanted John to direct it. After reuniting with Wilhite, however, the project stalled until finally Wilhite called it off when the funding had fallen through. (Wilhite subsequently completed the film, which was released through Hyperion Studios in 1987.) John was shocked and upset, especially after giving up, as he described it, "the greatest experience I'd ever had" working for Lucasfilm's Computer Graphics Division.

John called Catmull to break the bad news to him. Within an hour of his call, Catmull phoned him back with an offer to become a full-time employee of Lucasfilm. Starting in October 1984, John rejoined the division.

SEIZING THE MOMENT

Sensing the full potential of computer animation, John found himself in the ideal place and time to take this new technology to new levels as the computer opened up new horizons for him. As he told an interviewer, "I was never a great draftsman. I always got caught up in the single drawing and would become frustrated. The computer freed me to be a much better animator. I was allowed to think in an entirely different way."

In the early 1980s, the Computer Graphics Division also functioned to produce computer-generated visuals for live-action features—the Genesis planet effect for 1982's *Star Trek II: The Wrath of Khan* and the holograph sequence in 1983's *Star Wars Episode VI: Return of the Jedi*. After rejoining the division, John was given the opportunity to showcase his remarkable abilities with computer animation, working with Lucasfilm's special effects company, Industrial Light & Magic (ILM), this time on the Steven Spielberg-produced feature *Young Sherlock Holmes*. Barry Levinson directed this period adventure film that was lushly photographed in England. As a member of ILM's visual effects team under visual effects supervisor Dennis Muren, John, serving as the artistic supervisor, designed and animated the film's Stained Glass Knight character—a stained-glass window that transforms itself into a sword-wielding knight—putting advanced computer technology to the test by melding seamless computer graphics into a live-action sequence.

Creating many other computer-generated creatures meant putting the sequences on films, and ILM used its entire arsenal of techniques—dimensional animation, a souped-up system of stop-motion animation (called a go-motion system) using hand-crafted miniature puppets combined with live action via blue screen mattes, Rotoscoping, and a new method of compositing computer-generated images. Working in tandem with the Computer Graphics Division's technical director Bill Reeves, John helped push Lucasfilm's technology beyond what was considered "standard operating procedure." One of Levinson's concerns was *Young Sherlock* becoming too much of an "effects picture," so efforts were made to trim each shot down to prevent them from overpowering the production.

It was Muren, the sequence's creative director, who decided to do the Stained Glass Knight character as a computer-generated one and optically combine it in the film. For John and Reeves, developing an image that was familiar but menacing was a huge undertaking. It was the very first effect where the computer was used to make something that was meant to be real. They spent many long nights and all-nighters over a six-month period to complete the sequence that was composed of only six shots. "At first, no one was sure if this method would work," Muren recalled at the time. "I had all sorts of alternate plans if we had decided to back out of it. We had designs for a stop-motion figure. Another possibility was a rod puppet. Another was to do something in the animation department, or just go with a computer-generated outline. There were many bail-out points."

42 LEGENDS OF ANIMATION

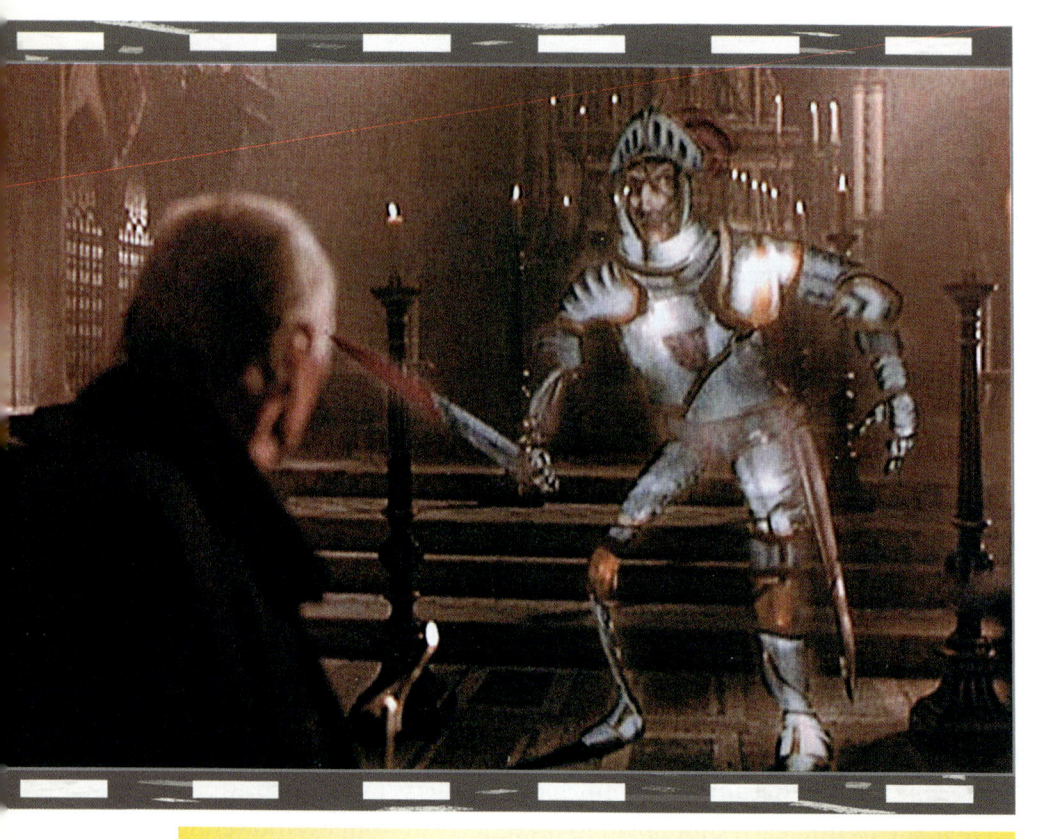

Lasseter's computer-animated Stained Glass Knight confronts a priest in a scene from Steven Spielberg's production of *Young Sherlock Holmes* (1985). © *Paramount Pictures. All rights reserved.*

The real conceptual problem was how to make the hallucinating priest who is confronted by the character be "afraid of glass? How can we make this thing look threatening and powerful?" Muren asked aloud. ". . . At the time, we still weren't sure if a computer image would work out."

As John told *Cinefex* magazine, "We were very concerned with making the character look organic—like an 18th century stained glass window that had actually popped out and come to life. We went through two or three different design phases trying to find something that worked. We even brought Eric Christiansen, who made all of the stained glass windows for Skywalker Ranch, and he gave us several suggestions. Incorporating what we learned in our research, Eric actually produced a small-scaled knight out of a real stained glass. Then, using that as a base, I built up clay on the original model to give more definition and curve to the pieces of glass."

To aid John in animating the character, Jeff Mann of ILM's model shop played the Stained Glass Man in a crude costume made of white cardboard, with footage of him shot in live action. John determined, without Rotoscoping him, how the scary knight would jump into the scene from stained glass in the church and start his walk. His design consisted of preliminary artwork from which Reeves keyboarded a model—an outline defining the parameters of the character—on the computer before entering the animation phase, the process of moving the artwork around on a cathode ray tube using the computer's paint box feature. During the rendering stage John also created a number of texture mattes—artwork made of bubbles and dirt and painted on a computer paint program—each to move along as the character walked and to give him its antique glass surface.

"Probably the hardest thing to do in that piece was to give the glass the look that it was old, beat up, dented—all these things that would be trivial if you did a model," John recalled. "With a model, you just paint it and light it. The computer likes things to be perfect. It likes perfect spheres and it renders them as if they were flawless. You can turn out a sphere like that! But to give it texture—to try and put a dent in a perfect sphere is so hard."

Opening in theaters on December 4, 1985, *Young Sherlock Holmes* was marginally successful despite its masterful blend of live action and special effects. For the film's amazing effects, John and the entire visual effects group were nominated the following March for an Academy Award in the category of "Best Visual Effects."

The experience of working with Muren, particularly his production management style, left a lasting impression on John. Assembling the entire team every morning to review dailies (raw footage of the production), he provided clear feedback and guidance regarding any changes that needed to made and why, and created an atmosphere best described as "one of collective problem-solving," something John, from his troubled experience at Disney, viewed positively and later incorporated into the creative culture at Pixar. As he once said, "The room was always open to discussion, and Dennis really listened to everybody."

After working on *Young Sherlock Holmes*, John chose not to stay with ILM to produce more computer-animated effects for movies. Instead, viewing himself as storyteller, he returned to Lucasfilm's Computer Graphics Division to produce what he loved doing most—cartoon animation. Things were about to change, taking him in that direction. His computer-animated accomplishments up to now would become the underpinnings of greater triumphs ahead to perfectly position him for the future as he championed computer animation in ways audiences around the world had never seen.

4

Championing Computer Animation Byte by Byte

As a small part of Lucas's overall corporate empire, Lucasfilm Ltd., the Computer Graphics Division had become a successful enterprise from inventing and manufacturing computer technology like its Pixar Image Computer and numerous applications in science, medicine, engineering, graphics arts, and entertainment. Founder George Lucas's original vision in creating the division was to use such tools purely for making films.

Subsequently Lucas's interest waned. He was not drawn to computer animation per se or interested in going into the business of making computers. After one sale fell through, Lucas found a buyer. He was Apple Computer founder and visionary Steve Jobs, who had been ousted as the company's chief executive officer in March 1985. Jobs saw the tremendous potential in the technologies they were developing with the ultimate goal of producing computer-animated cartoons and full-length films. So, in February 1986, he bought it for a fire-sale price of $5 million and injected another $5 million of capital into it. He promptly spun off the company and renamed it Pixar Computer Group (later changing it to Pixar Animation).

Relocating the company to nearby San Rafael from its former home at Lucasfilm in Marin, Jobs retained two original executives to head it—Ed Catmull as president and Alvy Ray Smith as vice president of research and development—and kept its research and development team intact along with its computer animation group, including John as director. Recognizing his immense talent, Jobs assigned John to write and produce groundbreaking computer-animated shorts and commercials. Right after Jobs spun off the company, he and his colleagues were told, "For the first year of Pixar, we want to have a film in the film show at SIGGGRAPH. You guys do it."

John and his cohorts Bill Reeves, Eben Ostby, and Sam Leffler did not have a film in mind right away that they wanted do. "So we all sort of did a little something. . .," John once related. "Bill was working on some interesting research on waves, so he did a little piece with waves. Eben was doing some procedural animation; he did something with a beach chair. And I was interested in doing things with lamps. I had done some student films with them, and they were kind of fun."

After creating the Stained Glass Knight sequence for *Young Sherlock Holmes*, John told Reeves and the rest of his group he wanted to learn more and "plunge himself into the thick" of doing computer animation. As Reeves commented to an interviewer, "A system can give movement to Mickey Mouse or Fred Flintstone or even Luxo Jr., but it still takes a storyteller to give it soul."

John began to work on his project using lamps, modeling one after a Luxo flex lamp. When texture and matte artist Tom Porter brought his infant son with him to work one day, John became fascinated by his proportions as the baby's head was much bigger than the rest of his body, and this struck John as funny. Afterward he began to wonder what a second lamp would be like as a baby. As he remarked in a published interview, "I scaled different parts of it down: The springs are the same diameter, but they're much shorter. The same with the rods. The shade is small but the bulb is the same size. The reason the bulb is the same size is because that's something you buy at the hardware store; it doesn't grow. So I animated it, and the story developed as I went on."

John's simple idea manifested into a fanciful story of two desk lamps, a father and a son, with armatures that swing around and bend and move in ways to give them personality. What he and his team achieved seemed unimaginable—taking two unlikely objects and giving them a sense of humanity that leaps to life memorably on the screen with believable and charmingly humanized characterizations—the father's dip of his shade, a sigh, and flick of his extension cord to convey his emotions, including calmly looking on as "Junior" vigorously plays with a bouncing rubber ball he pops only to return with a "bigger" ball. The result would become *Luxo Jr.*, John's most memorable creation to date and his second computer-animated short—only 2 minutes and 10 seconds in duration. He wrote and directed it, and Reeves technical directed and coproduced it with him.

Luxo Jr. was the first film John helmed using "procedural animation," employing the system Ostby had already developed to effectively handle this kind of animation on computers for the scenes of the ball rolling. Animating the scene was extremely difficult because he had to "match the translation with the rotation, and the size of the ball and so on. And I sat there with a calculator figuring all this out, and I realized, 'What am I doing? Computers should be able to do this.'"

John applied Ostby's system in future cartoons that he directed as well. In *Red's Dream*, for example, he employed the system in animating the unicycle's wheels turning and keeping the pedals flat ("All I did was do a pass, with the timing of it and the character moving around," John said) and in *Knick Knack* for the snow floating inside the globe of the snowman. "I just animated the character, and played with a few parameters, and the computer did all of the snow floating around. So as we go on, more and more tools are being developed. It's getting more and more power, but the animator still has the initial control, and we can still tweak it after the computer is done," he added.

Once again, John brilliantly employed sound effects for added effect, this time the handiwork of sound effects man Gary Rydstrom of Sprocket Systems, Lucasfilm's postproduction facility, with whom John had become close friends and whom he used for all of his films from *Luxo Jr.* on. "Sound has been very important to me. Actually

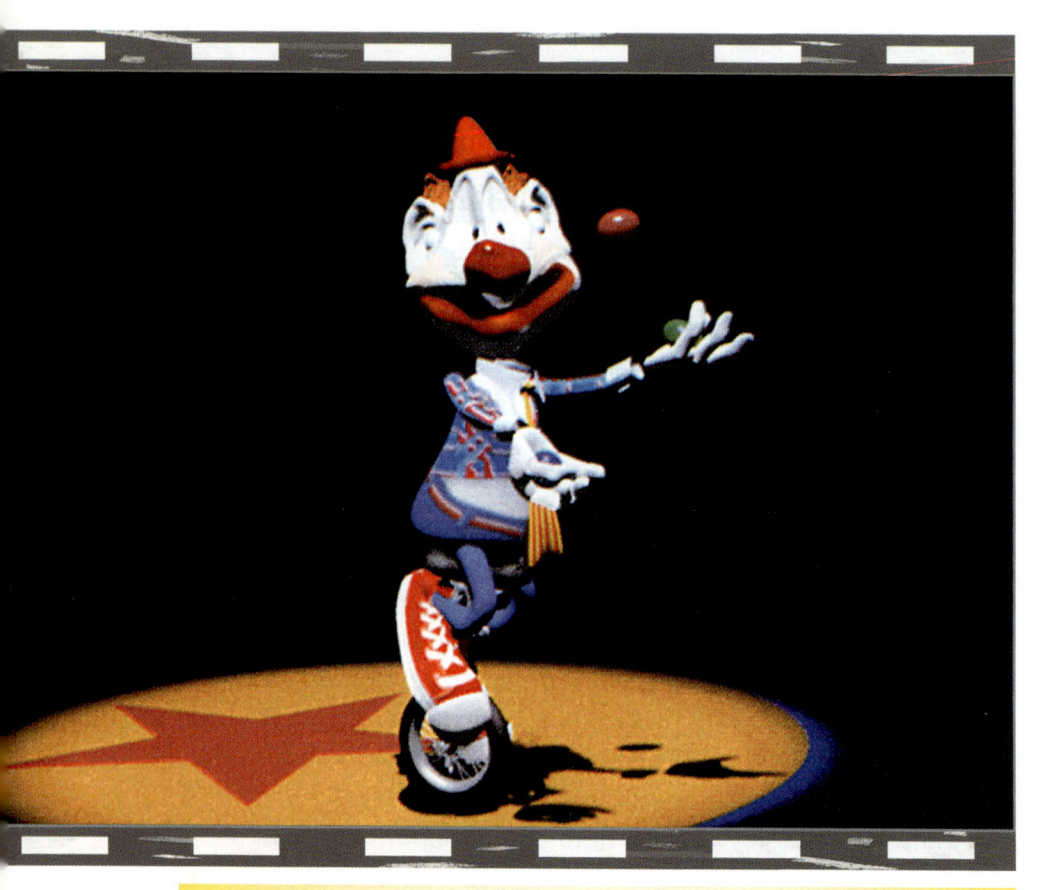

A scene from one of Lasseter's early computer-animated shorts about a unicycle dreaming of its days in the circus, *Red's Dream* (1988). *Courtesy: ARS Electronica. © Pixar. All rights reserved.*

back when I was a student and first began cutting sound effects to go with my animation," he explained. "I had this scene where a lamp was falling from a shelf and breaking its lightbulb. I was trying all these big crashes, and nothing was working. And I accidentally synched up the wrong sound to it, which was this little tiny minute little 'tink,' with this big camera jar and everything. I just cracked up because it gave it a completely different feeling. And in a way, it was that moment that I realized how important good sound effects were." As part of the process, John would meet Rydstrom ("a one-man band") before his storyboard was complete to review with him his initial ideas and "leave lots of openings in my animation" for him to do his stuff.

To complete the short in time for SIGGRAPH, John and Catmull worked around the clock with John taking a sleeping bag to work and sleeping under his desk, ready to work the next morning. Against all odds, they finished *Luxo Jr.* for SIGGRAPH and the time and effort they put into the project paid off. Premiering on August 17, 1986, at that year's convention in the Dallas Convention Center Arena, the reaction to *Luxo Jr.* was phenomenal and focused more on the film's content than what kind of software John used to produce it. The audience of 6,000 conventioneers had never seen anything quite like it. Before the colorful short finished playing, they were already on their feet giving the film a thunderous ovation.

After the showing, Jim Blinn, one of the early pioneers in the field of computer graphics, came running up to John and said, "John, I gotta ask you a question."

John's immediate thought was, "Great, here it goes. I don't know anything about these algorithms; I know he's going to ask me about the shadow algorithms or something like that."

Instead Blinn asked, "Was the parent lamp a mother or a father?"

It was the kind of reaction John was hoping for. "It's interesting; that question keeps coming up," John said in 1990. "A lot of people say it's a mother; a lot of people say it's a father. I always envisioned it as a father, but it's based greatly on my mother. To me, if it was a mother lamp, she would never let the baby jump on that ball. But the dad is like, 'Go ahead, jump up on it, fall off and break your bulb. You'll learn a lesson.'"

As he later admitted, "The thing I wanted to do in *Luxo Jr.* was make the characters and story the most important thing, not the fact that it was done with computer graphics. As you see in the film show at SIGGRAPH, a lot of times it's computer graphics for computer graphics nerds. People get excited about it purely because it was generated with a computer. I wanted to make a film for once where people who had never even seen a computer-animated film before would look at it and enjoy it as a film."

OPENING UP NEW HORIZONS

Either way, John succeeded. *Luxo Jr.* became a real breakthrough, sending "shock waves through the entire industry—to all corners of computer and traditional animation," Catmull later noted. "They did not realize that the computer was merely a different tool in the artist's kit but instead perceived it as a type of automation that might endanger their jobs. Luckily, this attitude changed dramatically in the early '80s with the use of personal computers in the home. The release of our *Luxo Jr.* . . . reinforced this opinion turnaround within the professional community."

Shown at animation festivals and in movie theaters, *Luxo Jr.* became the first widely seen short that used computer animation, creating a steady positive buzz wherever it played. In reviewing the innovative short, John H. Richardson of the *Los Angeles Daily News* wrote, ". . . within seconds, the audience is convinced the flex-lamps are father and son (or mother and daughter). Just the tilt of the flex-lamp's head speaks volumes about the relationship." Conversely, *Sacramento Bee* movie critic Joe Baltake, meanwhile, opined, "Lasseter takes a large high-tech desk lamp and a smaller, similar-looking lamp and casts them in the roles of parent and child, giving the parent lamp the bent-over posture and weary movements that come with trying to deal with a child, and the child lamp the itchy, irritating, destructive ways of a real-life kid. It's uncanny."

New vistas opened in his career, and as he traveled to animation festivals around the world where *Luxo Jr.* was screened, John could not help but marvel at the work of many Canadian, European, and United States animators whose films were also shown at these same festivals—some of the most honored artists of their time, including Paul Driessen, Bill Condie, and Cordell Barker—many of them greatly influencing him in his work. (Luxo Jr., by the way, would later become the mascot for Pixar Animation Studios, appearing in the company's logo before and after every film.)

John's latest achievement was soon recognized. Giving a nod from Hollywood about computer animation's place in making movies, *Luxo Jr.* became the first computer-animated film—and only American-made cartoon short—nominated that year for an Academy Award for "Best Short Film (Animated)" competing with just two others: New Zealand's *The Frog, the Dog, and the Devil* and Belgium's *A Greek Tragedy*, and losing to the latter. For the overtly enthusiastic 29-year-old animator-director, then living in San Rafael, and natural-born computer whiz Reeves, 35, a Berkley resident, receiving the nomination was more than they could have ever imagined. When the nominations were announced, John was in Europe on a train en route from Amsterdam to Paris and changed trains in Brussels to find the closet pay phone to call the Academy direct. Upon hearing the news, he started screaming and "All the Belgians just looked at me. There I was all alone with no one to celebrate with," he remarked at the time. "But when I got to Paris, I celebrated with friends and some good French champagne."

Later, in a much calmer state, he said, "For an animator, the Academy Award is the highest honor. This has been a goal—to be recognized by my peers."

Reeves, on the other hand, woke up to the news when his phone rang at 7:30 that morning and a friend told him of the nomination and his wife came running and gave him a big kiss. "It was a big surprise," he admitted

Reflecting on the importance of his achievement, Reeves later recalled, ". . . I knew at the moment that computer animation had achieved something that had never been achieved before; it was the story and the characters [that] were important in the film, not the fact that it was made with computer graphics."

They were informed they had to wear tuxedos, and neither John nor Reeves owned one. John bought his—a black tuxedo—for $45 at a thrift shop on Haight Street because, as he said, "I'd look stupid in powder blue. But I'll be wearing my black high-top sneakers, of course."

At that Monday's awards ceremony, in the face of defeat, they both thanked the team that had worked with them that made *Luxo Jr.* possible.

John found himself increasingly drawn to computer graphics because of the way such animation "can play with light," something impossible to do with hand-drawn cels. "A computer is like a pencil," he once noted. "It is really an amazing pencil. [But] computers don't create animation anymore than a pencil would create a drawing."

Fresh on the heels of this success, John turned out other award-winning shorts. A year later, he scripted and directed *Red's Dream*, one of his best works next to *Luxo Jr.*, with computer animation done in a more traditional Disney-like style. Combining great humor and heart-tugging moments, the film is reminiscent of Fellini's *The Clowns* in its depiction of a little red unicycle dreaming about his triumphant days in the circus. In Lasseter's version, a forlorn unicycle, Red, daydreams about his days performing in the circus with a schleppy little clown, Lumpy. Its current home is the discount section of a bicycle shop, Eben's Bikes (named after Ostby, a huge cycling fan), where it sits idle as other fresh-off-the-assembly-line shiny new bikes stand erect on the showroom floor awaiting a buyer.

The only Pixar short made with the Pixar Image Computer (a computer graphics designing system Pixar introduced in 1986 and redesigned a year later), the 4-minute and 10-second computer-toon was first shown in late July at the annual SIGGRAPH convention in Anaheim, California, in the shadows of Walt Disney's Magic Kingdom, Disneyland. Presented by Disney animation icons Frank Thomas and Ollie Johnston, the film drew an enthusiastic response from conventioneers. Released to theaters on November 30 of that year, the captivating cartoon was awarded the Silver Berlin Bear for Best Short Film at the Berlin International Film Festival that year.

A few years before at a SIGGRAPH convention, John met the woman with whom he would share his life: a dark-haired beauty, Nancy A. Tague. An applications engineer at Apple Computer, they discovered they had many things in common. One was their love of technology. A graduate of Carnegie Mellon University in Pittsburgh, she and her young son, Joey (born in 1980), soon became an integral part of John's life. Carrying on their relationship was not easy. John commuted north to the Lucasfilm group in San Rafael, and Nancy commuted south to Apple's headquarters in Cupertino, California.

John acknowledged Nancy's importance and contribution to his work early on. In his July 1987 article, "Principles of Traditional Animation Applied to 3D Computer Animation," which he wrote for *ACM*

Championing Computer Animation Byte by Byte   53

With photos of babies plastered on the wall behind him as inspiration, Lasseter works on animating and directing his film in which a toddler terrorizes a wind-up toy, his Oscar-winning computer-animated short, Tin Toy (1988). Courtesy: American Cinematographer

Computer Graphics magazine, he thanked her for her "ruthless editing" and Joey for "being pals and for telling us what happened in *Willie Wonka*." John's comment was in reference to a video Joey watched of the 1971 movie, *Willie Wonka & the Chocolate Factory*, as he worked on his paper.

In January 1988, Nancy served as an artistic director on a three-minute color film created in-house by Apple's Advanced Technology Graphics Group meant to display the capabilities of the company's new Macintosh II computer line. Produced by Galyn Susman, the film was called *Pencil Test*. John is credited with coaching Nancy as an animator and storyteller of the "Design Police" in the film. She also appeared on camera. Future Pixar director Andrew Stanton likewise served as an animator and storyteller on the project and helped produce its story.

John and Nancy were married that year.

By 1988, computer animation had surpassed being a novelty to becoming, as Jack Garner of *USA Today* wrote, as "common as the Statue of Liberty logo on NBC News or the water-and-mountain imagery of the surreal Prudential Life Insurance commercials." Storytellers and animators like John are aptly demonstrating that computer animation is "simply another tool for the creative filmmaker and not an end unto itself."

Later that year John topped his previous film but paid a small price in doing so. The newlywed workaholic animator moved into his office at Pixar, giving up the comforts of home and spending quality time with Nancy, who brought him clean clothes and fresh flowers during his voluntary confinement. He wanted to devote every waking hour to perfecting his latest computer-generated endeavor, which he wrote and directed and Reeves produced, *Tin Toy*.

After picking up their first Oscar nomination the year before, they focused on transcending the technological feats of *Luxo Jr.* with a spunky five-minute short packed with humor and emotion about a toy soldier's (Tinny) first encounter with a curious, free-spirited, drooling, diapered infant boy (Billy). It would become the first Pixar film to feature animation of a human character. John, then 32, got the idea for the film when he was sitting around watching videotapes, the '80s equivalent of home movies, of his baby nephew, Timmy McDonald, and Julia Reeves, the daughter of his colleague Bill Reeves.

As John recalled, "There was this great video of him [Timmy] chewing on this little rubber bat and just slobbering on it. The adults were all laughing about how the kids that age chew on their toys and someone remarked, 'They're cute little babies, all right, but how'd you like it if you were the toy?' Then I started to think from the perspective of the toy. People always say, 'Oh the baby is sooo cute.' But take it from the eyes of the toy, and this cute thing becomes a horrific monster."

SETTING THE BAR HIGHER

Tin Toy served as the "guinea pig" for Pixar's first testing of its latest technology, PhotoRealistic RenderMan, proprietary rendering software capable of creating 3-D images from outlines directly on the computer. Released that year, the rendering software became a major success. It was used to create the landmark special effects in director James Cameron's 1989 live-action film, *The Abyss*, and then *Terminator 2: Judgment Day* and Steven Spielberg's *Jurassic Park*, providing Pixar with a steady source of revenue from sales and licenses to third parties. It quickly became an industry standard, used extensively to augment live-action films.

Tin Toy was also the only Pixar short rendered on the RM-1 computer, based on an earlier rendering machine that was never sold publicly. Many bugs had to be worked out as they stretched its capabilities to the fullest in animating the film entirely by computer. But the creative pair took everything in stride, leaving the drawing to John and the programming to Reeves, who joked at the time, "I can't draw worth beans." John, smiling, countered, "I can't program worth beans."

Collecting more footage of babies at play—nine hours' worth—to study, John made some sketches and refined the story. Meanwhile Reeves, who also contributed to the design and construction of the backgrounds, created the models of the characters and fed the computer numerous geometric shapes, dimensions, and details to create the wire-frame images before animating them and creating a sense of warmth and realism for each character. Billy started as an oversized clay sculpture that John made by hand and sculpted into two parts—the body and then the head. Reeves made a 3-D model of baby Billy from the sculpture that he digitized on the computer and then merged with a skeletal description of the character. Accustomed to building characters through geometric shapes in their computer-animated films, the most challenging part of the project for him was to convincingly capture fluid movements of the human character baby Billy. Reeves, who holds a Ph.D. in computer science and never expected to end up making movies, spent hours researching facial animation, including "The Facial Action Coding System" designed by psychiatrists, as a starting point to reflect the right expressions. He also used a digitalizer, a device that tracks points in space, to design more than 40 facial muscles required for the baby's facial expressions alone. John was careful in making sure the resulting characters were convincingly lifelike. As he said at the time, "They have to seem to live and breathe and think on their own."

To create realistic movement and expression of Billy on screen, John and his team also gathered pictures of babies in various emotional states, and they posted them on a wall for reference. As Reeves remembered, "We studied the babies' emotions and tried to get that same feel in Billy."

John completed the storyboards and was busy animating Tinny long before the baby Billy worked properly. Problems in making him function correctly and look realistic took more time to solve than anyone had planned for. "I still think if I had had two more months, I could have made Billy more lifelike," Reeves told *American Cinematographer* in 1989.

In making *Tin Toy*, John set the bar high from the outset. Besides pushing the programming skills of Ostby, Reeves, and others to the limit, he spent a lot of time staging the film. One of the common complaints about computer animation was that the camera went all over. To avoid this pitfall, John planned out the film to make the most out of his camera positioning. In fact, he developed as his team's rallying cry, "No unnecessary camera moves!"

Early on John held a staging party with *Tin Toy* animator and editor Craig Good for that purpose. "We cleared out a big area on the floor and we got together all our toys as stand-ins and we actually positioned ourselves on the floor where we thought the camera should be—just to see how things lined up," Good recalled. "We also had a postmortem on the film and we naturally found things we wouldn't do the same way."

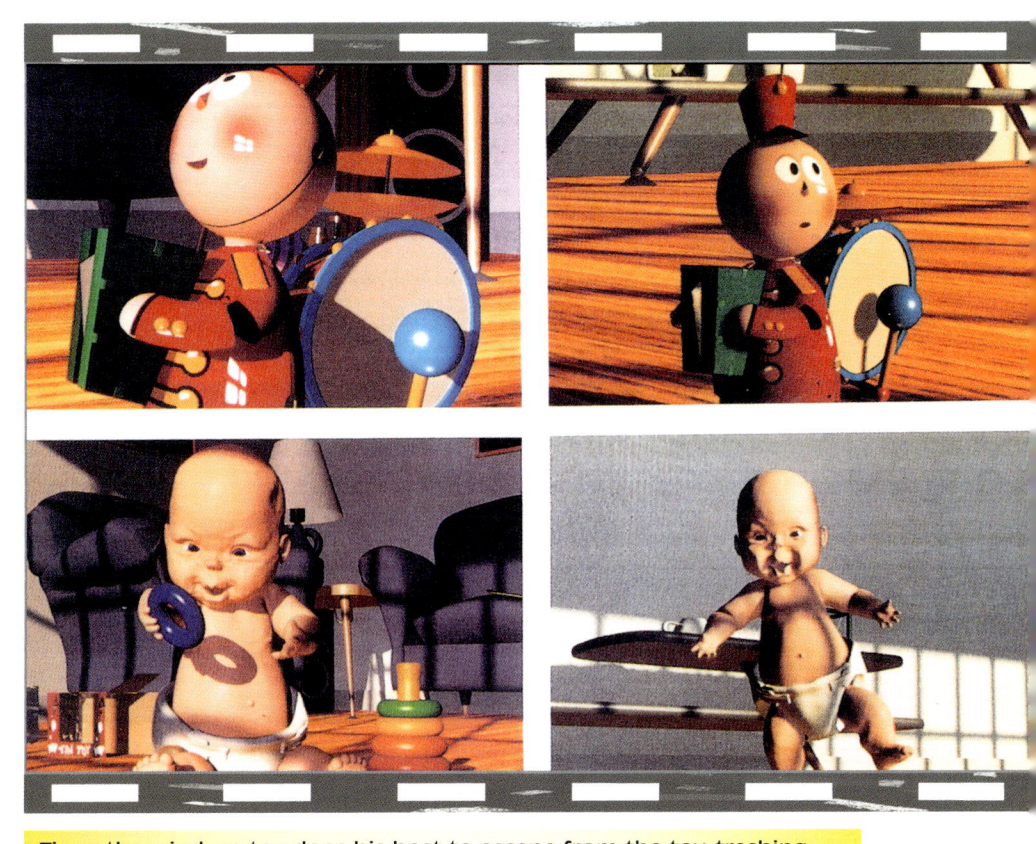

Tinny the wind-up toy does his best to escape from the toy-trashing toddler Billy in scenes from one of Lasseter's best Pixar shorts, *Tin Toy*. Courtesy: ARS Electronica. © Pixar. All rights reserved.

Contrary to popular opinion, doing *Tin Toy* in computer animation was not really more time-saving than traditional hand-drawn animation; if anything, doing human characters was much more complicated. "It's funny. Some of the easiest things to do in hand-drawn are hardest in computer, and vice versa. With computers, it's easy to do a three-dimensional rigid object and move it around, or to animate a room and move the camera within that room," John told a reporter. "If you try to do that in hand-drawn, it's really hard. Lighting is something the computer can do real well, but what you can do with drawn animation is get real organic, pliable, flexible characters and shapes and move those around."

Animating "organic" objects like baby Billy on computer was difficult at best. As John added, "It's something a computer doesn't really like to do. It likes things to be perfect. Draw me a sphere, that's easy, but draw me a sphere with a bump over here and a crack over here, that's hard. And deforming that over time, bending it, moving it around like a water balloon, that's really hard."

John had become much more comfortable working with computer animation, reaching the point where he could "think" directly into the computer, unlike when it first started when he would sketch out his story line and people were animating without any basic principles involved. "It's a very different set of tools," he told the *Columbus Dispatch*. ". . . Working with the computer is like telling an incredibly stupid person what to do. You're always translating. There are limitations; you learn to work within those limitations."

Once again John turned to Gary Rydstrom to create the film's wonderfully inventive sound effects. Rydstrom was cutting the sound effects for the live-action movie *Cocoon II* at the same time. It took him a day and a half to do one reel out of the eight or nine reels that made up the feature, but six weeks to complete the effects for *Tin Toy* because "He was so into it he loved it. He was doing it on his own time, and he kept layering and layering sound after sound. There must have been 20 different tracks for *Tin Toy*, and it really shows, because it's so rich," John later said.

In doing computer animation, John still considered sound effects important to the success of his characters to help give audiences a sense of something about them. As he explained, "I wanted the feeling with the lamps [in *Luxo Jr.*] that their bases were very heavy, so when they land it's with a thud, and so on. In *Tin Toy* it was very important to get a sense that the character was made out of tin, and that the baby was flesh and blood and much more massive. Sound really helps."

Producing *Tin Toy* took seven months, including a six-week period when John set up a futon in his office and literally lived there. In August 1988, two months after the release of Walt Disney Studios's highly praised *Who Framed Roger Rabbit* feature that cleverly combined live action with animation, a partially completed version of *Tin Toy* was screened at SIGGRAPH with great fanfare. At the same conference, Apple Computer's *Pencil Test*, the film Nancy had worked on, also premiered at the coveted SIGGRAPH Electronic Theater and was widely acclaimed as one of the best of the show.

Reaction from the trade show audience to John's *Tin Toy* and the escapades of Tinny trying to escape from the highly destructive baby Billy was thunderously positive. In October 1988, the completed version, containing 55 shorts and running a minute longer than *Red's Dream*, premiered at the Ottawa '88 International Animation Festival before being released to theaters in late December. "My greatest reward for all this is having the audience react," John said then. "People absolutely went nuts."

The results on screen were delightfully entertaining. The short tells the story of the first encounter of a small wind-up one-man band, Tinny, and his new owner, Billy. Initially enchanted by his babbling and the strange noises he makes, the small toy soon becomes terrified as the toddling monster chomps and trashes his other playthings before setting his sights on him. The slightly unsteady Billy chases after him. Sweet little Tinny seeks refuge under the sofa, joining the ranks of an entire troop of toys cowering in fear. In the end, Tinny bravely sacrifices himself to keep Billy from crying. The cartoon delivers on all levels. In particular, it produces the kind of warmth, realism, and expressive lifelike characterizations that John had endeavored to accomplish. It is remarkably detailed, funny, and poignant for a computer-animated short.

After Pixar burned through around $50 million invested by Jobs in its first decade, producing critically acclaimed but commercially unviable computer-animated cartoon shorts and selling very few computers, *Tin Toy* marked an important turning point for Pixar and John's career. Critics and audiences alike were effusive in their praise. John had been dubbed "the auteur of computer cartoons" earlier that year, and many who marveled at his work noted, "The first thing anyone notices about a Lasseter cartoon, however, is that it doesn't look like it was made by a computer." As one critic said, "It's difficult to believe that *Tin Toy* was achieved through computer animation, so three-dimensional do the baby and the toys seem." Another said, "Lasseter is a rare talent in the field of computer animation—someone able to use state-of-the-art computer technology to the fullest while infusing it with real emotion and humor." Spike Decker, co-organizer with Mike Gribble of the annual Festival of Animation, which screens the year's best collection of independent cartoon shorts in theaters across the country, added that "there is nothing that parallels Lasseter's work. His imagery is so lifelike and so steeped in human emotions that the viewer is unaware that *Tin Toy* was conjured on a keyboard."

John credited his feel for characterization to his experience as a traditional animator at Walt Disney Studios, where personality and characters are hallmark in their animated films. "Characters are the most important thing in my films," he said. "My big goal is to entertain the audience. If the audience is too aware of the technology, you defeat the very purpose of what you're doing. People won't believe in the characters, the way they move and feel—their personalities." As he added, "The technology that we use to create—it's not important that the audience is wowed by it. We want them to be wowed by the story or by a memorable character."

Following the positive reception of *Tin Toy*, John was excited about the nature of computer animation and its future. "It's new and right now it's like climbing a mountain no one has climbed before," he stated. "The baby was a tremendous amount of work, but it was thrilling because we were achieving new things."

Still it had become clear to John that the easiest things to do in traditional animation were the hardest to do in computer animation and vice versa. In traditional animation, there were no limits to creating "a squishy, deformed character" with drawings but to a computer, doing that was more complicated. "It doesn't deal with just a line drawing," he said. "It needs a three-dimensional form and a squishy form is hard to define—that's why Billy the baby in *Tin Toy* was so difficult."

Defending the artistic nature of computer animation, Lasseter often stated that although computers created the animation, somebody had to run them. "Computers are just fancy pencils," he later stated in an interview with the San Diego *Evening Tribune* in 1990. "I work hand in hand with the computer guys. I could not do this stuff on my own."

WINNING HIS FIRST OSCAR

In the end, John's and Reeves's efforts paid off. The technically sophisticated *Tin Toy* earned them their second Academy Award nomination, and became the first computer-animated film to win the prestigious award for "Best Short Film (Animated)." The film also won the Golden Nica Award at Prix Ars Electronica of the Austrian Broadcasting Corporation. On March 29, 1989, at the 61st Annual Academy Awards, held at the Shrine Auditorium in Los Angeles, the surprised tuxedo-clad duo was jubilant as they took the stage to accept the first of many Oscars to come. Reeves admitted the day after to feeling "dazed" after walking on stage to accept the award with John. "You don't know what's going on," he said at the time. "You hope your automatic pilot works, you hope you don't fall. I was a little stiff, but once we got offstage it was just hugging and kissing, that type of thing. Almost unbelievable."

The win, however, was bittersweet, as Academy rules permitted only two nominees per film in the animated-short category, so their fellow technical director Eben Ostby was denied recognition.

Winning their first Oscar represented a major historic milestone for the computer animation industry as it had never received the coveted award. The honor was indeed more remarkable since Pixar's entire computer animation team (known as the Animation Production Group), in a company of 140 employees that primarily manufactured software and hardware products for computer graphics and image processing, was made up of seven full-time workers. An unusual mix of business and artistry, the studio took on, as John once conceded, "a life of its own," after *Luxo Jr.* was awarded the company's first Oscar nomination and other awards. As he stated in an interview following the success of *Tin Toy*, "Computer animation doesn't change animation by itself—animators do that. I see computer animation as being able to stretch the medium of animation."

Lasseter and Bill Reeves hold up their Oscars for photographers in the press room after winning the award for "Best Film Short (Animated)" for *Tin Toy*. Courtesy: The Academy of Motion Picture Arts and Sciences/Margaret Herrick Library Collection.

Of his computer-animated shorts so far, *Luxo Jr.* remained John's favorite, "without question." Although *Tin Toy* won him his first Oscar, he once admitted he wished "the baby had been a little more cute," but since the point of the story was about a baby monster, "it worked really well, in fact; it may have been better since the baby looked kind of bizarre, than it might have if the baby was really, really cute." As for *Red's Dream*, he liked the film's sad ending but generally realizes most people's favorite is *Luxo Jr.* because "it's just this little simple thing, and it's complete on its own."

Discussing the distinguishing elements of his work, John told a reporter, "One of the things that is different is the fact that the work we do is in the story line and the personality of characters. Also, we're very concerned with the quality of the lighting, the quality of the surface. We do a lot of what they call texture mapping, where you can take the image and put it over any of the surfaces of the object."

As a result, John became a favorite—like "royalty"—on the animation festival circuit, where his films won more coveted honors at the San Francisco International Film Festival, the Zagreb World Festival of Animated Films, the International Animation Festival, and dozens of others. Though it did not contain one iota of computer animation, he found the Disney's live-action and animated feature *Who Framed Roger Rabbit* "thrilling to see" and "brilliant" in its technique, and what many in the animation industry had longed for: a cartoon that would generate that "kind of crowd reaction." The robust business and box-office clout the film generated clearly opened the door for many more animated features to be financed and produced out of Disney, unlike before when, as John said, "you couldn't get one financed if your life depended on it."

In May 1989, as his latest animated creation continued to delight audiences, John and Nancy welcomed a second son into the world, Bennett. In anticipation of the big day, two months before his birth, John chuckled as he told a reporter, "Really, I'm looking forward to it."

In the next few years, their family would grow from two sons to four with the births of P.J. and Sam. They would eventually add a fifth son, Jackson.

In the meantime John focused his energies on an incredible technical challenge before him: writing and directing his first computer-animated short in 3-D, *Knick Knack*. (In the film's opening credits, the title is spelled *knick knack*.) The first four films that he had made were primarily funded as technical test pieces of some aspects of new technology and stand as some of the finest examples of computer animation ever produced. Unlike those efforts, where all the animation created on computers was three-dimensional but viewed on two-dimensional monitors, this time around, John and his crew used 3-D monitors that required special glasses to actually see their work in 3-D. "This stuff is truly 3-D, it's really great," he said in talking about the project. "Luxo hits a ball, it bounces off the screen, he leaps forward and sticks his head out of the screen!"

Knick Knack, which is about an anxious snowman who tries to break out of his snow globe to join a fun party and a hot-looking bathing beauty, demonstrated John's unique vision and style as a writer, director, and animator. More "cartoony" than his other films, this hilarious 3-D stereoscopic film is a gag-driven throwback to Chuck Jones's *Looney Tunes* and to Tex Avery's cartoons at Warner Bros. and MGM, the pace and humor of which few animations had since equaled. "After *Tin Toy*, we really wanted to do a cartoon," he said. "I went back and looked at my collection of Chuck Jones and things . . . it was a very conscious decision."

Featuring an easy-listening original music score by Bobby McFerrin and marking one of the last cartoons John would personally animate, *Knick Knack* premiered in August 1989, at the SIGGRAPH Animation Show. This was before it was distributed theatrically in normal flat prints in late November. It was never seen in 3-D in movie theaters because projecting it in three-dimensions required a special setup with a silver screen and polarized projectors. John was typically humbled by how audiences reacted, saying, "It's surprising the reaction that it's getting."

Later, after Pixar allied with Walt Disney Studios, *Knick Knack* was re-released to theaters in 2003 with the premiere of Pixar's computer-animated feature *Finding Nemo*. For the cartoon short's rerelease, in a conscious decision to make the film more family friendly, John resized the breasts of both the Sunbather and Mermaid. Of the sudden change,

Championing Computer Animation Byte by Byte 65

An anxious snowman tries breaking out of his snow globe to join a fun party and a bathing beauty in Lasseter's stereoscopic 3-D short paying tribute to the likes of animation legends Chuck Jones and Tex Avery, *Knick Knack* (1989). © *Pixar. All rights reserved.*

he stated in the book *The Art of Pixar Short Films*, "It wasn't big bad Disney coming in and insisting we do this . . . it was our own choice. It was just crossing the line for me personally as a father, so I made the decision to reduce (these characters') breast size."

After Pixar appointed him vice president of creative development in 1990, John remembered his promise from his days at Disney to create a more collaborative environment if he was ever put in charge, and he kept his word. To this day, the soft-spoken animator follows a management style refreshingly different from the executive-driven environment he experienced at Disney. His style is a display of his kid-at-heart sensibilities, easily dispensed bear hugs, and openness to others' ideas that allows them to succeed without limits. Perhaps the clearest indication of his playful and casual nature is the way he dresses—in jeans, sneakers, and Hawaiian shirts (a love for which started in 1987) and his office décor. Surrounding him are collector toys from his youth including a stuffed, pull-string, voice-activated Casper doll on a shelf near his desk. It is the same doll he used to clutch at bedtime like a security blanket when he was a toddler ("My mom told me I never went to sleep without this guy," he later recalled) and his original childhood Etch A Sketch.

John and his creative team live by a simple mantra: They view themselves as storytellers first and computer animators second and maintain both a kid's and filmmaker's perspective about their work. Technically, he also asks of them that the images "not look computer generated." As he later told Peter Burrows of *Business Week*, [Filmgoers] are willing to give me a little portion of their life, so I want to entertain them. I don't want them to be bored."

As John mused, "I've often heard people say that managing creative people is the hardest thing in the world. They're never happy, they drive up the cost of things, blah blah blah.' I just manage people the way I always wanted to be managed. That is, to be creatively challenged, but never to be told what to do."

Looking to the future, John expressed a strong desire to make a computer-animated feature for Pixar someday, something he and his colleagues had long dreamed about making, taking computer animation to the next level. After winning his first Academy Award for *Tin Toy*, he and producer Ralph Guggenheim, who had been with the computer graphics company from its beginning, decided the time was ripe to move toward doing features. In 1995, Guggenheim remarked, "I started working with the people who are now at Pixar 17 years ago. And for 17 years were saying we're going to make films like this one day. . . . We thought a lot about how we were going to make this computer-animated film doable on the computer. And John, to his credit, said from the very beginning, 'This is not about making a film on computers, this is about making a film. Let's do that first and foremost.' So we went about writing the very best story we could and creating the very best characters we could, without regard to the technique. In live-action films, nobody writes a screenplay thinking about what focal-length lens they're going to use or how many feet of dolly track they're going to need, so why should we have limited ourselves in that way?"

Applying computer animation in longer form was something John looked forward to achieving. As he told an interviewer, "Ever since I've been with the group, we've been researching and developing computer animation systems, and with my influence it's very important to have computer animation systems that are developed for traditional animators to use. It takes quite a lot of training, but the tools are there that people are used to. And we want to get into longer forms of animation."

That same year John started experimenting with doing dialogue with computer animation, another step toward doing features, as "the dialogue I've seen with computer animation has been pretty weak," he said. "There are all these principles and things that over the years people have developed with animating dialogue. At Disney, they teach you certain things, and I'm real interested in applying those to computer animation as well, like I've applied the other principles of animation, like stretch and squash, and anticipation, and timing and so on."

Though computer animation was largely different than traditional hand-drawn animation, John envisioned in the next 10 years combining both art forms to do character animation and backgrounds by hand and by computers. As he added, "The technology we're developing is going to make it a lot more feasible to do that sort of thing, so it blends together better than in the past. Cel animation looks so different than computer animation, but I think with developments like what we did in the *Wild Things* test, and like in *Roger Rabbit* the shading that they achieved, you'll be able to make cel animation look a little rounder, more like you can do with computer animation."

Soon John would get his wish, and the results would be nothing short of extraordinary.

5

Toying His Way to Infinity and Beyond!

In setting the creative foundation for Pixar, John had established a reputation for himself as one of the leading animators in the industry. After directing two Oscar-nominated shorts and winning one Oscar, he became the talk of the entertainment community and one studio was not blind to his success: his former employer, Walt Disney. In fact, Disney's Michael Eisner and Jeffrey Katzenberg made overtures to woo him back into the fold. But John politely declined.

"I wasn't making much money," John explained, "but I felt I was on the edge of something. We were on the cutting edge of this new technology."

Besides, he added, "I was having too much fun."

Eventually Disney snagged their man, but only after taking a much different route. By the end of 1990, Pixar moved to new $15 million digs in a one-story office building on Canal Street in the Point Richmond Tech Center in Richmond, California. The high-tech mini-studio was located in a highly industrialized area within earshot of railroad tracks along which trains rumbled daily, shaking the screens of millions of dollars worth of computers. With Pixar Chief Executive Officer Steve Jobs realizing that sales of the company's RenderMan software and other tools were not enough to fund its technology research and film projects, he pushed forward with the idea of using Pixar's technology to make money by developing television commercial campaigns for clients. In late 1989, after Pixar had entered into a contract with San Francisco production house Colossal Pictures, for the purpose of making commercials, John and his crew began work on Pixar's first television commercial. For Tropicana Orange Juice ("Wake Up"), it starred a computer-animated drinking straw. Afterward Pixar accelerated its pace in producing more commercials, with John directing many other successful television ads in 1990, starting with boxing Listerine bottles, which helped generate much-needed revenue for the company. John also helmed commercials for other major clients, including the California Lottery, Pillsbury, and Volkswagen.

Later that year, confident enough in Pixar's progress in making short films and commercials, John had conversations with Disney about producing a film based on *Tin Toy*. Aligning Pixar with Disney made sense. The two companies had already been working together since 1987, after jointly developing a highly sophisticated, computer-assisted animation process, called the Computer Animation Production System (CAPS). Disney first used the process in 1987 to digitally ink and paint animators' drawings and create three-dimensional backgrounds in its smash hit *Little Mermaid* (1989), and its first all-computer animated short, *Oilspot and Lipstick*. They again paired it with traditional animation to produce dazzling effects in two other blockbusters hits that followed: *The Lion King* (raising the dust scene) and *Aladdin* (flowing lava scene). Riding high on the success of its animated movies, Disney CEO Michael Eisner and studio chief Jeffrey Katzenberg were primed to invest in this burgeoning new technology.

At a meeting with Katzenberg, including Catmull, Smith, Reeves, and Jobs, John pitched doing a sequel to his Oscar-winning short, *Tin Toy*, as a half-hour computer-animated television special, called *A Tin Toy's Christmas*. He and Pixar's entire animation brain trust viewed the project as a stepping-stone to convince Disney or other film studios they were capable of tackling a feature film. Given Disney's bad reputation and his past history with the studio, John was reluctant to work with them and had to be convinced it was a good idea. Katzenberg dismissed the idea of doing a special. He was more interested in making great films and building up Disney's production of animated features. The meeting ended with Katzenberg intending to do features with John and Pixar that Disney would distribute instead.

John pitched another toy-related concept to Katzenberg as a possible feature in February 1991. This was a month before Pixar laid off 30 of its 72 employees, including Jobs, after five years of consecutive losses. Everything but development of commercials and RenderMan was shut down. During this difficult time John pitched a concept that was well ahead of computer-animation capabilities of the time and unlike the standard Disney fare: the tale of a hand-me-down toy that is a child's favorite until he gets a brand new and very fetching toy for his birthday. Thus the movie *Toy Story* was born.

Walt Disney Feature Animation Executive Vice President Thomas Schumacher, who was directly involved from the start in its development, conceded that "it is an interesting idea on the surface." Katzenberg was enthusiastic about the project. Afterward John and his animation group created a brief "proof of concept" scene of Woody knocking Buzz Lightyear off the top of the dresser. When they showed it to Disney, it instantly sold the executives on the project. Agreeing to terms on May 3, 1991, the cash-strapped Pixar signed a three-film deal with Disney in early July. Under the terms of the deal, Disney would fund the production and promotion costs and Pixar would earn a modest percentage of the box-office and video sales gross revenues. Pixar's share of the film profits were estimated between 10 and 15 percent. In exchange, Disney retained 100 percent ownership of the films and characters and sole licensing rights for toys and merchandise. Pixar retained the rights to any direct-to-video sequels, and data files and rendering technologies employed in their films. The deal orchestrated by Katzenberg also called for John to write and direct the first film.

Pixar's new agreement with Disney marked its full foray into the computer age in feature animation as its films were still animated primarily by hand, a laborious and expensive process. *Toy Story* producer Bonnie Arnold later recalled, "The deal that Pixar made with Disney was that they would deliver a G-rated movie. But right from the start,

Disney asked us to go after the broader audience and put the emphasis on the humor."

Despite Katzenberg's enthusiasm, however, other Disney executives were highly skeptical. "They didn't think you could get the emotion out of the computer-created characters," Walt Disney Studios Chairman Dick Cook recalled. "When something new comes out, you're always going to have a certain amount of skepticism."

CREATING HIS FIRST COMPUTER-ANIMATED FEATURE

With only a few dozen people on staff, Pixar quickly geared up by hiring more people to begin design and development of the production as John commenced with turning his concept into reality. With his natural affinity for things "silly and fun" coupled with his tremendous grasp of computer graphics technology, John was ideally suited to write and direct the film. Set in "a world where toys have a life of their own when people are not present," according to a Pixar press release issued in July 1995, *Toy Story* became the first full-length feature in history made entirely by computers and software. The high-tech company's latest project was yet another indication of Hollywood's increasing reliance on computers and its technology for entertainment-related uses and how new computer-animation technologies were changing the way movies were being made.

Instead of solely authoring the screenplay and keeping all creative decisions to himself, John assembled a core group to work collectively on production. It became part of his management style of bringing together the best minds and talent—or so-called brain trust, as they became known—starting with *Toy Story*. Thus he was one of four writers credited with developing its original story that took three years to write. He and two members of Pixar's 12-person creative team, Pete Docter and Andrew Stanton, came up with a treatment based on Joe Ranft's original story. Then Joss Whedon, who did a major rewrite for the live-action movie *Speed* and last-minute script doctoring for Kevin Costner's *Waterworld*, came aboard and laid down the foundation of the story much more in depth. That became the framework they worked from for the next three years in scripting the story. After carefully studying a ton of animated films and live-action films, such as *Thelma and Louise, The Odd Couple, The Defiant Ones, Midnight Run, 48 HRS., Butch Cassidy and the Sundance Kid*, and many others, they turned to a concept that worked well in live-action films as the basis of the story—a "buddy picture"—with hip and irreverent humor to appeal even to the toughest teen audience. "The buddy movie always appealed to me," John explained, "because characters grow in the movie."

Admittedly John and his cowriters had no idea if what they were putting down on paper, in some cases, was actually possible to be captured on computer, for example, creating skin, hair, and cloth for the characters. But during the next three years technology caught up, making the improbable within reach. Most members of *Toy Story's* crew who worked alongside John were in their twenties and thirties, including Guggenheim and fellow producer Bonnie Arnold, a veteran of live-action feature film producing who had joined the production. Arnold compared creating the film to "the peeling of an onion in the sense that you work very hard in one layer of the film at a time," she said.

Disney was "encouraging from the start," as John once said, but they were also worried that the subject of toys would be "too juvenile." As he recalled, "They wanted a movie adults could relate to, as well as kids, and so Andrew (Stanton) and I and our creative team went into a think-tank mode and took a look at what toys really mean to people."

From the beginning, John said, "I'm a toy lover and I thought there was a great potential there—beyond just for kids, but for adults as well. But we didn't want to do [a typical Disney cartoon] story. They were doing these musicals, love stories, villains, all this stuff. We wanted to do something different."

Much of the story evolved from sessions held in a secluded room at Pixar, where John, Docter, Stanton, and Ranft recalled their childhoods. During one such session, Stanton revealed he once strapped an M-80 to his G.I. Joe toy and blew him to pieces. (This later became fodder for the sequence introducing the bully-on-the-block Sid who trashes his playthings.) "I treated my toys a little nicer," John said at the time. "It always bothered me when neighborhood kids would take their G.I. Joes and throw them around."

Katzenberg was heavily involved in the story review process and Disney was still very much an executive-run studio as when John had worked there. John and his creative team met with him and other executives sometimes once a month, sometimes more, and sometimes less, to creatively review different parts of the story. During meetings, Disney had one development executive walking with a clipboard, and every time John and his team pitched an idea, they had to report back on how they were addressing the notes.

Katzenberg gave them extensive notes and, above all, wanted them to "make it edgy, make it edgy, make it edgy," so the film and characters would play to adults as well as kids. At other times, after explaining how they had perfected a sequence, an executive would say, "Well, you know, it could use a little of this."

"They always had a feeling that no one—well, no adult—was gonna want to come and sit and watch a movie about kids playing with toys," John said. "So we followed their notes."

John's colleagues at Disney, *Aladdin* directors Ron Clements and John Musker, told him and his group, "That happens to us on every one of ours, too," where the characters were not working or empathetic and situations were not set up right. Trying to appease Disney, they had to throw out the whole second half of *Aladdin* and start over, part of the process of what Disney called "finding your film"—the story that gels and grabs audiences that has little to do with technique. Consequently John and his team "beat our heads against the wall" for months, Guggenheim added, to find the common thread to the story that would keep people interested, delaying the animation while they worked to get the story right.

Finally, on January 19, 1993, Katzenberg approved John's and his cowriters' "Roy Rogers versus Buck Rogers" script. Under John's supervision, he had prototypes of the movie's main characters created by a bevy of concept artists he had hired, including children's book illustrator William Joyce (of *George Shrinks* fame) whose original concepts for Woody and Buzz Lightyear were never used. Next he proceeded with

Lasseter directs Tim Allen, the voice of Buzz Lightyear, during a recording session for *Toy Story*. © *Walt Disney Pictures. All rights reserved.*

storyboarding and producing and editing preliminary footage of the story with rough music and dialogue of the actors. For the characters' voices, he set his sights on Tom Hanks for Woody because, in his words, he had "the ability to take emotions and make them appealing" and Disney's Tim Allen as the macho superhero Buzz Lightyear (cast during the second season of his top-rated ABC sitcom, *Home Improvement*). The Oscar-winning Hanks related instantly to the pull-string cowboy. At their first meeting John showed him a computer-animated Woody with his voice lifted from the motion picture *Turner & Hooch*, in which he starred. Hanks howled with laughter and asked, "When do we start?"

John showed the test footage to Katzenberg, along with a room full of art work for the movie, and he agreed Hanks was right for the part.

Afterward John went about creating story reels—or a rough draft of the film—matching recorded dialogue of Hanks, Allen, and other actors to hand-drawn story sketches in the place of finished animation. The reels would be Disney's first chance to see the story on screen.

BACK TO THE DRAWING BOARD

On November 19, 1993, hereafter referred to at Pixar as "Black Friday," John, Guggenheim, and Arnold brought the first reel to show Peter Schneider, president of Walt Disney Feature Animation. Schneider had been involved from the start in helping to seal the deal between Pixar and Disney. Following Katzenberg's directions to make the film less juvenile, more edgy, and more adult, the results were disastrous. Woody and Buzz bordered on unlikable. The pull-string cowboy Woody was nasty and the toy-bashing character Sid was nightmarishly brutish. Schneider immediately questioned the creative direction of the film. "Guys, no matter how much you try to fix it," he told them, "it just isn't working."

As Tom Schumacher, then Disney's executive vice president of animation, later recalled, "We pushed them too far. They interpreted us wrong and made the film too abrasive. It lost a lot of its charm."

Schneider ordered the three of them to shut down production immediately. Determined to keep his production crew of 20-odd people together, John begged for time to fix the first reel. "Let us do one more cut, give us a couple more weeks," he pleaded. "Let us see what we can do ourselves."

Schneider gave them just two weeks. It was a hairy time for John. His stomach was just in a knot and he thought, "Oh, man, I can't do this!"

Following the debacle, while meeting with Joe Ranft and Pete Docter, John told them, "Screw it, let's just make the movie we want."

John and his creative team retrenched and worked hard on making Woody and Buzz likable and memorable. They hammered out a revised story line, which Disney helped rewrite. At the end of the day they arrived at the film's look, style, and performance.

"We had a good idea of what our movie was about," Guggenheim said. "We were struggling with some issues and trying to find out other things, and we talked to [songwriter] Randy [Newman] about writing a song about friendship. . .He came in a few days later and sat down and played `You Got a Friend in Me' that is virtually unchanged from what he played for us. We all sat there and went, `My God, he got it better than we ever thought we got it!' It was such a defining moment." (Newman, incidentally, wrote three songs for the film and has provided additional musical scores for other Pixar films since then.)

The final story that appeared on the screen was developed in what John called "wild group gag sessions," some lasting for days, from which he and his creative partners determined, "Toys live to be played with by kids, and anything that prevents that from happening will make a toy miserable, desperate, an emotional wreck. Or a hero," he said.

By February 1994, Katzenberg approved the revised script that made Woody more sympathetic, with production starting up again in April. John knew he had won over Katzenberg the moment he said, "Buzz and Woody are working great, but let's look at the secondary characters."

John was then well on his way to having all the pieces come together in perfect harmony that Disney would support. "The toys may be playthings, but they operate in an adult world with a sense of function and purpose," John later said. "Every toy has a personality, from the plastic T-Rex who looks ferocious but is timid because he's so ridiculous looking with his pathetic little forearms, to the Mr. Potato Head who's a bit of a control freak to compensate for the fact that his facial features are always falling off."

Directing *Toy Story* was a huge technical challenge for John. Not only did he and his team have to perfect the characters and story to appease Disney, but Pixar also had to greatly expand its computer processing power, memory, and staff. In addition, they had to come up with animation software that their increasing number of nontechnical artists could easily grasp to produce the final product. At one point the entire production was shut down until their engineers and technicians were able to create software to resolve such computer processing shortcomings. At the time Pixar had originally agreed to its deal with Disney, the technology that was in place was ideal for making computer-animated commercials and five- to six-minute shorts like *Luxo Jr.*, but not longer formatted productions like feature films. So they had to, as Schumacher described, "pioneer the whole rest of the look of the film from that point on."

This blip in the production pipeline did little to shake Disney's confidence in John and his staff, however. "I was mostly concerned with the story, the characters—how it all played as a movie," Schumacher added.

Computer-generated imagery proved particularly appropriate for animating the inanimate objects foregrounded in the movie. The new technology allowed John's crew to re-create the textures and three-dimensional quality of actual toys while bestowing them with human traits through expert character animation. First they storyboarded the story, then 3-D models of each character were crafted, and all the actors' voices were recorded before the computer work could begin. As John described it, "Computer animation is a bit like puppet animation. You can use CAD [computer-aided design] techniques to create a set on the screen, then you place characters in the set. You do it frame by frame, just like any animated film."

Every character they created based on their respective 3-D model was then programmed into the computer and given a complex field of controls to make them come alive. Animating characters like Woody and Buzz required more than 700 individual animation controls—called "avars"—to create all the nuances of body language and facial expressions to make the characters appear convincing, as animated by a crew of 27 animators, most of them veterans of other mediums, specially trained to use Pixar's software technology. "When I was looking for animators," John once stated. "I looked at guys who worked with clay, cel, sand and pencils; no matter what the medium, I wanted to see if they were able to take a character and make us feel that it was breathing and thinking."

Additional technical artists then added textures, colors, and lighting to virtually every toy, building, furnishing, and so on that was designed and artificially generated from scratch. Each frame was then rendered on a floor-to-ceiling stack of super-computers in a temperature-controlled vault—Pixar's "nerve center"—the place where all the creativity was finally processed. Rendering one frame took 20 hours of computer time alone. Changing and adapting shots was definitely much easier than it would have been for a cel-animated feature, where making minor alternations would require massive redrawing. "With the computer, you can tweak things until the cows come home," John said. "Everything is controllable.

While working on the movie, John's team of animators ran into some novel problems, however. At one point in the film, the marionette-like Woody and space ranger Buzz sneak into a fast-food restaurant camouflaged in a milk shake cup and burger box. In their first scene together, Woody's head poked through the cup's plastic cap and Buzz's through the box's cardboard top, something that was not planned and was the result of an error in the process of computer animation as their movements and scale had not been precisely coordinated. The error was corrected with only a few keystrokes, not hundreds of revising drawings, as with traditional hand-drawn animation.

John and the studio pulled off producing *Toy Story* with only 110 artists, far fewer than the some 500 to 600 needed to make Disney's hand-drawn spectacle *Pocahontas*, with technology that provided a distinctive and vibrant 3-D look and texture and detail otherwise impossible to re-create frame-by-frame using traditional animation methods. Making the movie took a staggering 800,000 machine hours and 110,064 individual frames—with a single frame containing more than 1.4 million individual pixels—to create. Even then John was not about to suggest that computer animation—which he called a "new medium" within the art form of animation—would replace tradition animation anytime soon. "It can do things that no other medium can, but there are also certain things that it's much more difficult for computers to do," he noted. "If you look at the great Disney classics—for instance, the Dwarfs in *Snow White* are a real tour de force of drawn animation.

Toying His Way to Infinity and Beyond!

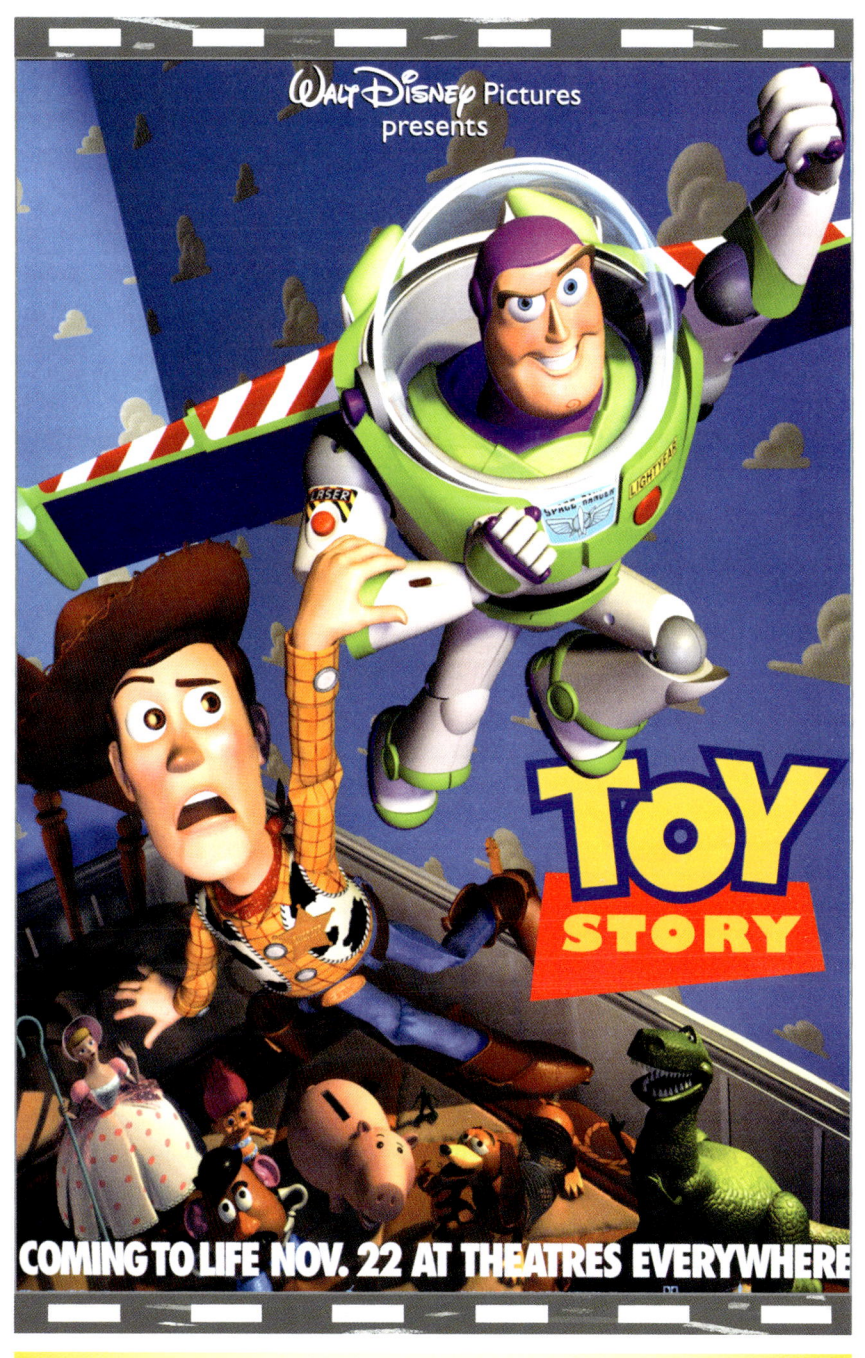

Full-color trade advertisement for the November 1995 nationwide premiere of *Toy Story*. © *Walt Disney. All rights reserved.*

The sloppiness of Dopey, the clothing and all of that, that is very difficult to do with a computer."

Trading conventional cel animation for the power of computers to replicate the expressions and movements of toys in a three-dimensional environment, the finished $30 million film took four-and-a-half years to make and required the equivalent of a thousand CD-ROMs of storage space to produce. It afforded the luxury of being able to easily store and retrieve everything on demand for reproduction instead of having to strike the set when production was finished. Despite all the talk of the film's technological revolution, for John, the real strength of the film was its appealing characters and story line. As John stated prior to the movie's release, "In the end, that's what audiences are really entertained by."

Naming the movie was indeed a family affair. John used his four boys as his audience for his films. He would bring home early versions of his movies and show them to them and "just watch the boys watch the movies," he said. "If they get bored, I know it's not holding. I listen to them talk about it afterward.

John's oldest son, Joey, then a high school freshman, convinced him on what the film should be called. "Originally it was a placeholder name, just generic," John explained. "Disney hired people to come up with every possible title. We went through 600 names, and Joey said, `What's wrong with 'Toy Story?'"

In 1992, the Lasseters moved to the Sonoma wine country after previously making their home in Redwood City and San Jose. Nancy wanted a small-town atmosphere in which to raise their children. By the late spring of 1993, they somehow squeezed out time between John's busy schedule to design and build their rambling, family styled, Victorian-reproduction house that became home to them and their four sons, ages 3 to 15. Far removed from the Hollywood glitz, their boys shared two bedrooms and had their own playroom stuffed with toys and games. Enjoying their expansive new surroundings also were two pet chinchillas and a family mutt dog, Max.

John found that living there helped keep him grounded. As he later commented, "Our friends are a salesman, contractors, dentists. Going to soccer games and Cub Scouts and Little League, it helps keep me personally aware of the audience I make these movies for."

Protective of the normalcy he shared with his family, little could prepare the 38-year-old animator for the onslaught of publicity and celebrity that would follow. As he told a reporter, "I'm not interested in me, myself becoming famous. I'm interested in my work becoming famous. I've been working on this film for four years. It's like this child you've raised and are now sending off into the world."

VAULTING HIM TO THE TOP OF THE CARTOON WORLD

Teamed with Disney's seemingly bottomless promotional budget, *Toy Story* was first hyped that summer in theaters with a movie trailer that was sort of *"Top Gun* meets *Toy Story"* to overcome the notion the film was only for kids. Everything after ranged from 50 million plastic giveaways of Burger King's Kids Meals to interactive CD-ROMs to a Christmas parade at Disney World. The attention vaulted John, after 16 years of respected work in film animation, and Pixar to the top of the heap. As a holiday offering, expectations for the film were enormously high. In an interview with *Fortune* magazine, Steve Jobs, Pixar's board chairman and majority stockholder, trumpeted the movie as "the biggest advance in animation since Walt Disney started it all with the release of *Snow White* 50 years ago." He added, "If *Toy Story* is a modest hit—say $75 million at the box office—we'll [Disney and Pixar] both break even. If it gets $100 million, we'll both make money. But if it's a real blockbuster and earns $200 million or so at the box office, we'll make good money and Disney will make a lot of money."

Three weeks before *Toy Story*'s world premiere, John was busy with last-minute technical work and doing press junkets and juggling preproduction for Pixar's second and next computer-animated feature in a three-film contract with Disney. As a gift to school kids, on November 11, he previewed *Toy Story* in his new hometown at the 325-seat Sebastiani Theatre benefiting the Sonoma Valley Education Foundation, which provides funding and support for public school programs.

Moviegoers paid $50 to $150 a head in this tiny wine country town to rightfully boast they saw it first. Including a preshow cocktail party, the screening co-opted all the trappings of a huge Hollywood premiere. Huge klieg lights beamed into the heavens as high school schools kids, acting like paparazzi with box cameras, eagerly snapped flash pictures of guests, some costumed as their favorite celebrities, arriving in stretch limos. Greeting them on the red carpet were ushers wearing 1930s and 1940s dresses.

The event marked the first time a film had been previewed at the historic Sebastiani Theatre since 1941's unveiling of *The Sea Wolf*, starring John Garfield, Ida Lupino, and Edward G. Robinson. With two of his sons attending Sonoma public schools at the time, John, who hosted the event, saw the preview as a way of sharing the rewards of the project he had labored over since 1991 with his community. "I have had the idea ever since I moved to this town," he told the *Press Democrat*. "We just love Sonoma."

His wife Nancy handled promoting the event, including designing the posters, with Disney supporting the small-town fund-raiser in style by picking up the cost of printing 6,000 fliers, posters, programs, and tickets, and daily giveaways of *Toy Story* tie-ins: Frisbees, T-shirts, yo-yos, refrigerator magnets, candy bars, and other T-shirts bragging, "I Saw It First." Disney also donated a special Dolby sound system to the Sebastiani for the occasion. John collected hordes of *Toy Story* collectibles signed by the film's stars to sell at a silent auction after the preview, with proceeds from the event topping $20,000, almost three times the foundation's budget from the previous year.

On November 19, six days before Thanksgiving, Disney held the "real" world premiere of *Toy Story* at the El Capitan Theater in Hollywood. In a display of excess even by Disney standards, they transformed the three-story building next door into a "Fun House" theme park to hype the holiday movie. Two weeks before its release they trumpeted its arrival with a four-page ad in *The Los Angeles Times*. One by one, stars such as double Oscar-winner Tom Hanks and comedian Tim Allen arrived on the carpet amid all the pomp and circumstance. John, more comfortable garbed in untucked Hawaiian shirts and sneakers, wore a

Hugo Boss jacket that a friend's sister had brought him specifically for the occasion. He and Nancy sat smack dab in the middle of the audience, where John nervously watched to see if audiences loved his "toys" as much as he did.

Three days later *Toy Story* opened at more than 2,400 screens nationwide. Putting wide smiles and looks of amazement on the faces of small children and teenagers spilling out of theaters across the country, the 78-minute romp became not only a fabulous exercise in computer wizardry and a visionary achievement but also an immediate success. While kids clearly enjoyed the adventures of Woody and company, grown-ups also responded to the witty parable whose heart is based on "a love of toys." It is Andy's sixth birthday and his favorite cloth and plastic-faced cowboy with a pull-string voice, Woody, immediately becomes jealous of a fancier, brand-new toy his boy owner is given as a present: a jut-jawed, space-age, action hero with a built-in voice, pop-out wings, and laser beam, Buzz Lightyear. The spaceman instantly riles up Woody and the rest of his platoon of plastic toy friends living in Andy's room when he replaces the cowboy doll as Andy's new favorite. The rival heroes ultimately bond, however, after becoming trapped in a milk crate in the room of a sadistic neighborhood bully, Sid, a known toy torturer who delights in disassembling his toys. They settle their differences and become friends in the end.

Voice performances by an outstanding dream cast—Hanks as Woody, Allen as Buzz Lightyear, legendary put-down comedian Don Rickles as the insecure and sputtery Mr. Potato Head, Wallace Shawn as the sensitive and neurotic T-Rex, Jim Varney as Slinky the Dog, Annie Potts as Bo Peep, and John Ratzenberger (best known as Cliff the mailman on *Cheers*) as the know-it-all piggy bank, Hamm—only buttressed the illusion of the film's toys-come-to-life story line. Audiences flocked to see it. Taking a mega-bite out of the box-office pie, by the end of the holiday weekend the G-rated movie—blurring the line between traditional animation and mainstream movies—grossed nearly $40 million and, in its first 12 days of release, $65 million at the nation's multiplexes. On the following Wednesday after its debut, Pixar stock went public at $22 a share and closed its first day of trading at $39, making

Jobs, who held 80 percent interest in the digital studio, a billionaire in one day—at least on paper.

More importantly, as the first computer-animated feature, *Toy Story* won universal critical raves from critics from coast to coast. Writing in *Time* magazine, Richard Corliss called *Toy Story* "the year's most inventive comedy" and concluded that, "when a genius like Lasseter sits at his computer, the machine becomes just a more supple paintbrush." *Newsweek*'s David Ansen, on the other hand, praised the film as "a winning animated feature that has something for everyone . . ." with animation that "pops off the screen with a vibrancy that's totally unlike traditional hand painted animation." Owen Gleiberman, writing in *Entertainment Weekly*, declared, "I can hardly imagine having more fun at the movies than I did at *Toy Story* . . . the miraculous new Disney feature that's the first full-length animated film to be produced entirely on computer." Film critic Rita Kempley called the film "irreverent, ingenious . . . the picture offers an eye-popping parade of 3-D-seeming anthropomorphosis, but it also has enormous humanity and heart."

Such critical reception was only the prelude to the movie's success. That year, under John's direction, *Toy Story* became the highest grossing film of the year—raking in more than $192 million in the United States and more than $362 million worldwide, though most of the profits went to Disney as producer and distributor of the film. The vast digital library of textures, images, scenes, and characters were also easily adapted for equally successful licensed products, many of them bestsellers in their own right, including a video game for 16-bit Genesis and Super Nintendo systems, an interactive screen saver featuring 40 scenes from the film, and animated television series, among other projects, based on the movie.

In the months that followed, John spent little time with his family in their Sonoma home, logging thousands of miles jetting across the United States, Europe, and Asia plugging *Toy Story*, which was dubbed into 30 languages. During one of his junkets he was pleased to see his entertaining and amiable characters, Woody and Buzz Lightyear, gabbing in Swedish on the big screen and delighting audiences. He was also deeply touched by one scene he witnessed: a young boy at the Dallas airport clutching his Woody doll, waiting for his father to come off the plane. "The look on his face was pure joy," John said. "He was so proud of his Woody doll. I realized these characters don't belong to Pixar; they belong to the world. I always think of that little boy."

Overall John swore he never made movies to impress the tech industry and animation world but to give the whole family a movie they could enjoy. "I jokingly say we don't make these movies for someone to see one time through," he said. "We make it so there is something for the parents suffering through this for the 100th time on video."

Needless to say, with his dazzling family-friendly film embraced in every country, it was no surprise that *Toy Story* won a multitude of honors, including two Golden Globe awards for "Best Picture – Musical or Comedy" and "Best Original Song." The film was also nominated for three Academy Awards for "Best Musical or Comedy Score," "Best Original Song," and "Best Original Screenplay," written by him, marking the first time an animated feature had been recognized in that category. The Academy's Board of Governors honored him that year with a Special Achievement Oscar "for the development and inspired application of techniques that have made possible the first feature-length computer-animated film."

Despite already owning one Oscar for his 1988 "Best Animated Short" *Tin Toy*, John was flattered by the board's decision to award him a special Oscar. As he stated prior to the ceremony, "Of course I'm pleased. The Special Oscar is a tremendous honor. They don't give it often, I think only twice. The purpose of it is so they can award an award that has no category." For the splashy star-studded March 1996 event, John sported his own tuxedo. Reciting and toiling for days over his acceptance speech, he kept it characteristically concise. John was accompanied to the Southland by Nancy and his four children, who watched the doings from their grandparents' home in the Los Angeles area.

That April, John and Nancy celebrated John's Oscar win by throwing a lavish invitation-only party at Kunde's Wine Waves in Kenwood, a small suburb outside of Sonoma. Approximately 247 guests were on

Lasseter holds the golden statuette special achievement Oscar awarded to him in 1996 for his inspired leadership of the Pixar team on the first-ever computer animated movie, *Toy Story*. © *Associated Press*

hand to fete John, including several fellow Oscar winners, among them eight-time winner Dennis Muren from Industrial Light & Magic and four-time victor for special effects Gary Rydstrom from George Lucas's Skywalker Ranch. Highlights of the evening included a giant ice sculpture of Oscar, John's two Oscar statuettes dressed as Ken and Barbie in a tuxedo and prom gown respectively, free-flowing Kunde wines, and huge, ample boxes of cigars for those attending.

On November 21, almost a month after *Toy Story* (in Spanish and English versions) and *Tiny Toy Stories*, a collection of five computer-animated shorts John made in the 1980s, were both released on DVD, John and *Toy Story* swept all eight top motion-picture honors at the International Animated Film Society's annual Annie Awards, including "Best Animated Feature" and John winning "Best Director."

Box-office revenues together with video and licensing fees for *Toy Story* brought in about $1 billion for Pixar and Disney, unprecedented for an animated movie. Earlier that spring John squelched rumors that a *Toy Story* sequel was reportedly being rushed to video. "That's way too premature. There's been no strong discussions or decisions made," he said. "We hadn't even really thought about a sequel. But I'm sure there are people who want to see what happens to Mr. and Mrs. Potato Head after they got together."

Despite the film's runaway success, John remained true to himself—humble and modest and unchanged by his sudden fame and success—becoming something of a mentor to young animators interested in the world of computer animation. His advice to those seeking to jump into the fray was, "Don't get so seduced by the technology that you forget to learn the basic design" and, as he added earnestly, "Study the old films."

Though John missed the thrill of hand-drawn animation, he was comfortable working with the organic, complex imagery of computer animation and his stature in the industry. As he stated, "I like being a pioneer, pushing the medium."

While enthusiastic about this lively art form, he was ever aware that the advancements in computer wizardry, as evident in *Toy Story*, marked the discovery of a brave new world that would only become an even greater force in the future. "Ten years from now," he predicted, "technology will be so complex that *Toy Story* will seem simple in comparison."

The question now before John and Pixar was, "What could they do for an encore?"

6

Living in a Pixar World

With the success of *Toy Story* eclipsing even Hollywood insiders' best predictions, Pixar awarded John a $1.25 million cash award and bonuses based on revenue of future films. Much of the responsibility for the company's fortunes rested on his shoulders and those of his animation team. His new arrangement followed Walt Disney Co.'s announcement on February 24, 1997, of a new five-year agreement with Pixar to coproduce five more computer-animated movies throughout the next decade as rival studios DreamWorks SKG, Warner Bros., 20th Century Fox, and Universal boosted their production of animated films to compete. Calling the coming projects "the essence of our company," Disney Chairman Michael Eisner added, during a news conference at the world-famous Disney studios in Burbank, California, "It all starts here. If it doesn't work here, everything else we do does not matter."

As part of the new deal, Disney committed to spend up to $48.75 million, buying one million shares of Pixar stock at $15 a share and warrants to buy 750,000 additional shares at $20 a share, and another 750,000 shares at $25 a share during the next five years, for a 5 percent stake in Pixar. After being approached by many other studios about entering into a partnership, Pixar CEO Steve Jobs fashioned a potentially lucrative deal with Disney. Sharing production expenses of their movies with Disney, they would equally split all revenue once they recovered their costs for making their upcoming films. They would also be partners in related products, including home videos and toys, clothes, and other merchandise based on the movies. More importantly, the movies would carry the Disney and Pixar brands, a move designed to establish Pixar as a premier movie company. As Jobs told reporters, "The collaboration we had on *Toy Story* was magical. The thought of working with someone else—we just couldn't imagine it would be as good."

Besides retaining John to steer its animation team, Jobs kept Pixar's core management intact as well, including Executive Vice President Ed Catmull and Chief Financial Officer Lawrence Levy. By that August the company forged ahead with plans to move its head offices and animation studio within the next two years to a $22 million campus-style complex being built to house its 375 employees. Pixar had purchased the acreage for the site in Emeryville, California, for $5.8 million in May. During the maelstrom of activity surrounding Pixar's future growth and expansion, John oversaw three productions at once in different stages of development. One of these he was co-executive producing with Catmull was *Geri's Game*, Pixar's first new computer-animated short since 1989. Pixar had a goal of producing one or two shorts each year going forward.

Geri's Game was written and directed by newcomer Jan Pinkava. The 4-minute and 50-second film, released to theaters on November 25, 1997, follows the exploits of an elderly man, Geri (voiced by Bob Peterson) playing chess with himself. Taking two years to complete, the entertaining short was intended to help perfect new computer-animation techniques involving cloth and skin, which were extremely difficult to animate. It racked up more honors for the powerhouse animation studio. That included an Academy Award for "Best Short Subject (Animated)"—beating three others, *La Vieille Dame et les Pigeons*, *The Mermaid*, and Walt Disney Television Animation's first Oscar contender, *Redux Riding Hood*. The Oscar was Pixar's seventh overall since its founding in 1986, including scientific and technical Oscars awarded at the Academy Awards in February.

Two other projects that John was steering toward completion, both scheduled for release in 1998, were much more pressing and demanding of his attention. One was Pixar's first new computer-animated movie under its current deal with Disney. *A Bug's Life*, written and directed by John, was about the wicked world of creepy crawlies. The other project was a new direct-to-video sequel to *Toy Story*, due out in the second half of that year.

Tentatively titled *Bugs*, John's next big movie was to be a modern take on the popular Aesop's Fable *The Ant and the Grasshopper*. It involved the story of an ant colony that hires a flea circus to defend itself against food-stealing grasshoppers. As with *Toy Story*, John and his team jumped into it headfirst without any idea if what he had in mind was achievable. When he brought the subject up to his staff and told them, "We're going to make a movie about all these bugs," half of them responded, "We can't do that."

Ten times more complex to make than *Toy Story* and considered one of the most technologically innovative animated films of its time, *A Bug's Life* marked another giant technological leap as John promised it would, employing more powerful computers and software. The film became only the fourth computer-animated feature ever shot in widescreen CinemaScope, adding to the complexities in making the production.

Because *A Bug's Life* existed exclusively in the outside world—as opposed to the closed-in world of *Toy Story*—John knew that it was going to be a challenge re-creating the organic settings of the movie and giving them the detailed sumptuousness of the character's miniature world. "All the time we were doing the research and being inspired by the insect world, I wanted the audience to be reminded that this was a little world," he explained to a reporter. "A fallen leaf would be huge to them, or when an ant climbs up on a dandelion and floats down on one of the seeds, it's like he's hang-gliding." In creating an epic quality unlike anything seen on the big screen before, animators got on their bellies to look under plants outside Pixar's East Bay headquarters as part of their initial research. In fact, one of John's techie colleagues invented a tiny video camera, which they called the "Bugcam," and attached it to a stick with little wheels so they could roll it along in the grass and capture real-time images from underneath plants from half an inch above the ground. The footage provided a unique perspective of light and color intermingled beautifully in a world that appeared like it existed under stained glass. "You know, you just think of the ground as grass and stuff, but when you really get down in it and look up it's amazing how translucent that world is," John said. "It's like stained-glass windows in some of our scenes. We have the bugs enter a forest of clovers and it's amazing. It's so beautiful. They're like sequoias. That's what we can do now with the technology."

With so much of the film taking place outdoors in daytime, groundbreaking new software was developed to approximate natural light, shadows, and color tints. As Jobs said at the time, "*A Bug's Life* is denser than any animated film you've ever seen. The subtlety of the characters' facial expressions absolutely defines the state of the art, but the other things you'll see are autonomous elements. For example, we wanted to have the grasses and the clovers blowing in the wind. Well, if the animators had to worry about that, they'd never get to the characters. So we actually developed programs that make the grasses know how to blow by themselves."

Much more conceptually intensive, *A Bug's Life* also had more animated characters—12 main characters and a throng of hundreds of others—and more scenery than *Toy Story*, which took place indoors, so the backgrounds were flat and static. Whereas Woody and Buzz each had 750 moving parts with 135 facial controls in *Toy Story*, Flik, the main character, had 3,000 movable parts and 320 facial controls to bring him to life. Another challenge was developing new software to create large groups for a crowd scene involving 800 characters and giving each individual insect distinct looks. It worked so well that John expanded the number of crowd shots from the original 50 that were planned up to 460.

MAKING A MOUNTAIN OUT OF AN ANT HILL

Following its completion and leading up to its release, however, John and Pixar found themselves at the center of a major controversy. They

Living in a Pixar World 93

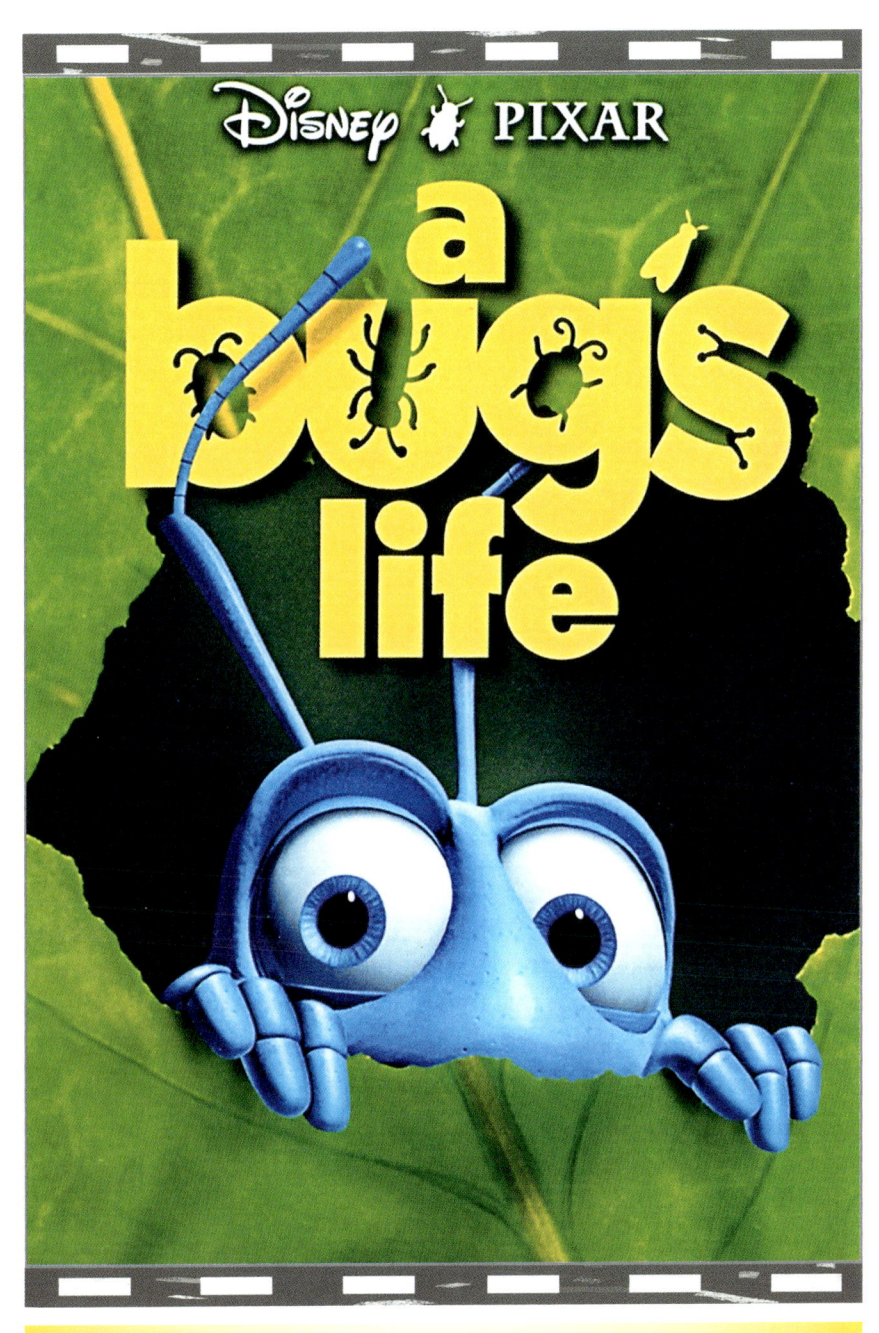

A poster publicizing Lasseter's second feature he codirected, *A Bug's Life* (1998). *Courtesy: Cinema Poster Archive. © Disney/Pixar. All rights reserved.*

were thrust into the uncomfortable position of defending themselves when word broke that DreamWorks Animation, headed by former Disney studio chief Jeffrey Katzenberg, was producing its own ant-related computer-animated feature, *Antz*. The Woody Allen-voiced lead effort was to be released on October 2, almost two months before theirs. As a result, members of the press raised questions as to how much Katzenberg knew about *A Bug's Life* before cleaning out his desk as Disney's studio chief to rush out his own rival insect movie at DreamWorks. Much off-the-record sniping among those involved in making both movies occurred in the background as both camps set out to publicize their respective films, but John took the high road when asked to comment. "We concentrated on making our film the best film we could," he stated. "We had been working on our film for about a year and a half when we found they were starting theirs. We were disappointed, but we concentrated on making our own film."

Declining to discuss the issue of the rival movies further, he added, "I would frankly just like to talk about our movie."

Just what Katzenberg knew about the Disney-Pixar ant movie became the subject of great debate. When examining the saga of the dueling movies further, Disney had long been considering doing an ant movie. It had had in development there, since around 1984, a film called *Army Ants*, and then retitled *Ants*, which went nowhere in three years. On August 25, 1994, two days after Katzenberg resigned, John, who was already working on *Toy Story* at the time, pitched his idea of *A Bug's Life* under its original title to Disney executives other than Katzenberg, including executive vice president of feature animation Thomas Schumacher, who greenlighted the project on the spot. John had no prior knowledge of "this ant thing we'd had that never went anywhere," Schumacher stated. "Of course, Jeffrey was still at the studio then, so he would have known [about *Bug's*]."

After resigning, Katzenberg stuck around to finish up old business, including seeing a rough cut of *Toy Story*, before finally departing the Disney lot on September 30. He then filed a $250 million breach-of-contract lawsuit against Disney that was later settled. On October 12, he joined forces with movie mogul and director Steven Spielberg and former record executive David Geffen to form DreamWorks SKG (the initials of its cofounders).

John remained on friendly terms with Katzenberg after his resignation. While in Los Angeles in October 1995, to oversee postproduction of *Toy Story*, he met with Katzenberg at his office at DreamWorks and excitedly told him about *Bug's*. During the exchange Katzenberg inquired at length about when *Bug's* was due out. Around this time Katzenberg was coincidentally looking for a computer graphics studio to acquire to produce computer animation and settled on buying Pixar's Northern California rival PDI. Shortly after the acquisition DreamWorks announced it was producing its own ant film, called *Antz*, after liking a pitch by DreamWorks studio executive Nina Jacobsen. It would be based on a story by Tim Johnson. By then John was well into codirecting his *Bug's* project. After learning the news of Katzenberg's competing project, he phoned him and said, "Jeffrey, how could you?"

As John told author David Price in his book *The Pixar Touch*, "He started talking about all this paranoid stuff about conspiracies—that Disney was out to get him. He said he had to do something. That's when I realized it wasn't about me. We were just cannon fodder in his fight with Disney."

Discussing the erupting controversy with the press, Schumacher explained, "Now, from this, you can take any number of things away. One is that we had been developing an ants story before John. He came up with his totally independently—and that happens all the time. It's also a logical conclusion that whenever you go into the three-dimensional world, insects are interesting. And there is a consistency of a small number of people who have known about all of these projects the whole time. Draw your own conclusions. But the point I want to make is, I don't find it unusual that someone would spontaneously think of it."

Even though they got a jump on production, it took John and Pixar four years to make *A Bug's Life* and Katzenberg and DreamWorks-PDI two and a half years to finish *Antz*. After announcing plans to make *Antz*, Katzenberg supposedly offered to kill his project if Pixar would stall work on theirs—which they refused—as releasing *A Bug's Life* at

Thanksgiving would directly compete with DreamWorks's cherished animated Biblical epic, *The Prince of Egypt*, due out that Christmas. Originally slotted for a March 1999 release, DreamWorks instead pushed up *Antz* to October, ensuring it would be the first computer-animated bug movie of the fall. John subsequently felt "betrayed" after leaning *Antz* was scheduled to open before *A Bug's Life*.

The preemptive maneuver by Katzenberg and his upstart movie studio by rushing out their first $85 million CG feature reaped a strong critical and box-office response, grossing more than $75 million in North America, making it the most successful non-Disney animated feature ever made. Publicly, John tried to spin Katzenberg's and DreamWorks's success as something positive. "I love good, healthy competition; I'm the most competitive person on the planet, and I think it's good for every industry," he said in an interview. "Our close friends at Industrial Light & Magic are doing their first computer-animated film of *Frankenstein*, and I am so excited about that. But what I love is to be challenged by other studios with fresh, original ideas."

Despite concerns over *Hercules* becoming Disney's lowest grossing animated feature, most industry analysts predicted that even if *A Bug's Life* fared no better than that it would still gross more than $100 million. *A Bug's Life* was first shown at a gala preview on Saturday, November 7, at the Sebastiani Theatre in John's hometown of Sonoma again to raise funds for the Sonoma Valley Education Foundation. The film later opened on Thanksgiving Day at Hollywood's El Capitan and movie theaters across the country. John's latest computer-animated triumph became an instant hit, taking in more than $46 million in its first 10 days of release and approximately $162.7 million in the United States, easily recouping its production costs of $45 million while surpassing DreamWorks's *Antz* with a worldwide box-office gross of $363.3 million.

Boasting a cast of well-known film and television stars, including Oscar-winner Kevin Spacey, *News Radio*'s Dave Foley, *Seinfeld*'s Julia Louis-Dreyfus, *Frasier*'s David Hyde Pierce, and the veteran voice stylings of Phyllis Diller and the late Roddy McDowall, *A Bug's Life* represented a quantum leap forward, technically and artistically, that delighted audiences. The movie's star power and technical breakthroughs were all secondary to the strength of its story of an inept worker ant, Flik (voiced by Foley), who saves his beleaguered ant colony after recruiting what he thinks are warrior bugs to fend off a gang of marauding, food-stealing grasshoppers. When they turn out to be a troupe of over-the-hill, circus-performing insects, he faces the grasshopper leader, Hopper, on his own, and thereby wins the heart of the queen-to-be, Princess Atta. In the end, Flik and the ants learn that their strength comes in working together, an underlying theme of the CG-animated epic.

The movie's artistry, lifelike characters, and stunning visuals were not lost on critics. As *People* writer Tom Gliatto wrote, visually, *A Bug's Life* "is perfect, a fully realized, richly colored world seen from the level of a blade of grass." *Time* critic Richard Corliss said, "As Walt Disney knew, animation is more than sublime trickery; the word means giving life. With a different kind of mouse, Lasseter does just that as his film finds its heat and heart." Corie Brown Giles of *Newsweek* found *A Bug's Life* "great fun," as well as the "giddiest, most inventive family movie of the year." Giles also went on to call the film "funny and silly and tender, full of fun scares and endless sight gags."

Variety reviewer Todd McCarthy was similarly impressed, noting that *A Bug's Life* "bursts upon the screen with beautiful verdant hues." However, McCarthy also felt that the movie is "a bit too busy at times and excessively noisy," a complaint echoed by Owen Gleiberman of *Entertainment Weekly*, who compared *A Bug's Life* to "a fireworks show that's too big and bursting to take in." Gleiberman concluded that this animated feature is "imagination overkill." *Nation* reviewer Stuart Klawans was more positive in his evaluation of the film, however, saying that "far from being a soulless exercise in technogreed, *A Bug's Life* jigs along cheerily, celebrating not only Flik's ingenuity but also such un-Disneylike virtues as eccentricity, urban disorder and the revolt of workers against alienated labor."

GOING BACK TO TOYS

Meanwhile John, who was promoted earlier in the year to Pixar's executive vice president of creative, proceeded with his planned sequel to *Toy*

98 LEGENDS OF ANIMATION

Lasseter served as producer on *Toy Story 2* (1999), featuring America's favorite cowboy Woody. *Courtesy: The Academy of Motion Picture Arts and Sciences/Margaret Herrick Library Collection. © Disney/Pixar. All rights reserved.*

Story. He faced an imposing problem: the curse common in Hollywood of producing sequels that are subpar compared to the original. Doing a sequel was a big gamble since only one animated feature film had spawned a theatrically released follow-up: Disney's *The Rescuers Down Under*. In bringing back the original cast—at a substantial increase from their original salaries—John and Pixar bucked the trend.

Talks of the sequel had immediately begun with Disney after the success of the original film. Disney proposed producing the sequel, however, directly for the home video market. Their plan was to follow the same successful template they had used in 1994 to produce *The Return of Jafar*, the highly profitable sequel to their blockbuster animated movie *Aladdin*. John and Pixar thought otherwise. They felt the production deserved to be, as author Karen Paik wrote in the illustrated Pixar history *To Infinity and Beyond!*, "more than the direct-to-video rush job that had been originally planned." Pushed back from its late 1998 release, John got his wish. Disney signed off on producing the film on a much grander scale.

John originated the idea for the sequel after his four sons ransacked his toy collection while visiting him at his studio office, which was filled to the ceiling with toys of every shape and description. "I loved to have them visit, but every time they came in here, I was a nervous wreck," he once admitted, "because a lot of the stuff is one-of-a-kind or autographed or collectible. I would find myself telling them not to touch things. And that made me think, 'John what did you learn from *Toy Story*? Toys are put on this Earth to be played with by a child!'"

Over lunch one day John discussed with Pete Docter the proposition of doing a sequel—how the original movie featured a "heaven and hell" for the toys in Andy's and Sid's rooms and "what purgatory would be," as Docter said. The conversation segued to talking about John's kids and the toys in his office. From that encounter he devised the concept of the sequel to be titled *Toy Story 2*.

Originally *Toy Story 2* commenced production as a 60-minute video sequel. Resulting from internal conflicts and personnel changes and a shrinking pool of experienced story people and animators to staff it, the task of producing it was turned over to a secondary production team as John and Pixar's primary creative team worked hard on finishing *A Bug's Life* simultaneously. After working nonstop to complete the original movie, *Toy Story*, and then *A Bug's Life*, most staffers were exhausted and ready for a break from being "behind the eight ball for a change," stated Pixar editor and director Lee Unkrich. As a result, the first completed reels of *Toy Story 2* failed to live up to the same standards as the original. They came across as the cheaper secondary effort of a direct-to-video production that John and Pixar had wanted to avoid in the first place. Except for Disney executives who were impressed by its in-progress imagery, many Pixar staffers were likewise unhappy about how the sequel had turned out. That was until John was able to take corrective action and turn all of his focus on the project after *A Bug's Life* was released.

After taking his family on a press trip to Asia and returning home, they all suffered from a severe case of jet lag and insomnia. So he and Nancy gathered all their sons into their bed and watched *Toy Story*. A year and a half had lapsed since he had last viewed the film. Seeing the characters and remembering how proud he was after finishing the first movie, the next morning he went to his office and viewed the development reels of *Toy Story 2*. "And it really wasn't very good," he admitted. "I felt like the wind had just been knocked out of me."

John and Pixar met with Disney to inform them that the film had to be redone. Executives disagreed, saying there was not enough time to remake the movie before its scheduled released date. Deciding they could not allow the film to be released in its existing state, Disney asked John to take over the production. Disney gave Pixar nine months to complete the entire film. John immediately recruited the same creative team behind the original, including Andrew Stanton to write a new script, Joe Ranft to co-supervise the story department, and Lee Unkrich, who had edited *Toy Story* and *A Bug's Life* and had become one of his closest creative collaborators, to codirect the film with him and Ash Brannon. He asked Pete Docter to help redevelop the story. Once John told them, "I'm going to take this movie on," none of them wanted to see the second *Toy Story* fail. They all found the motivation from within to give another 100 percent even when there were days when they did not think they had it in them.

John called together the entire story crew for an emergency two-day summit in Sonoma to rewrite the script. While sitting around the table, he came to the realization as they started laughing hysterically at the ideas that emerged that *"Toy Story* was us." They came up with the foundation, the basic story, and plot points that weekend. Afterward, the story crew rewrote and re-storyboarded the whole film in a month—an unprecedented achievement, especially for a full-scale animated feature.

Despite the enormous pressure he was under, John stayed true to himself. During a Los Angeles recording session for *Toy Story's* music, he displayed his sentimental side. He surprised Nancy and had "Happy Birthday" sung to her by the 105-piece Hollywood orchestra on the Sony sound stage. The stage had once belonged to MGM and music had been recorded there for many great musicals, including *The Wizard of Oz* and *American in Paris*.

Revamping and completing *Toy Story 2* severely affected many of John's crew. The frenzied and brutal pace of the production left many people physically and psychologically spent. Some employees developed repetitive stress injuries from working nonstop for nine months straight on a keyboard and mouse. One was left permanently disabled. During a wrap party for employees and their loved ones at the Castro Theatre in San Francisco, John was well aware of the heavy toll the film had taken on everyone. Overwhelmed as he took the stage, he said, "We are never going to do this again."

Just in time for the holidays, on November 24, 1999, *Toy Story 2* opened in 3,236 theaters nationwide. The story was about friendship, loyalty, and values. While Andy is at Cowboy Camp, his favorite toy, Woody the pull-string cowboy, ends up in a yard sale when one of his arms gets broken. Considered a highly valued collectible, an obsessive toy collector steals Woody and prepares to put him behind glass for good. During his captivity, he discovers his illustrious past as the star of a '50s western television show, *Woody's Roundup*. Woody learns he is the "pièce de résistance" in a collector's set based on the show, including his spirited costar, Jessie the Cowgirl, left behind in a garage sale when her child owner outgrows her. Risking life and limb, Woody's space-age friend Buzz Lightyear and their band of other toys ultimately come to their rescue and the toys are reunited.

Any fears John had that the sequel could not live up to or surpass the original were instantly quelled. During the Thanksgiving weekend, the 92-minute, G-rated adventure, made at a cost of $90 million, tallied $57.3 million, an average of $17,734 in ticket sales per theater in three days and $80.1 million since its Wednesday premiere. Eventually *Toy Story 2* made $245.8 million domestically and $239.1 million overseas for a stunning total worldwide gross of $485 million. It went on to become the third highest grossing film of 1999, far outdistancing the original. In 2000, the continuing toy saga also became the biggest box-office smash of the year in the United Kingdom and helped accelerate moviegoer attendance in the country to its highest in more than 25 years. Ticket sales topped more than 143 million that year.

This second time around, John's efforts won widespread acclaim from critics, many of whom considered *Toy Story 2* better than the first—a rare feat in Hollywood. "This film continues the work of its predecessor," wrote film critic Janet Maslin in the *New York Times*, "making sure that computer-generated animation will never be the same." Kenneth Turan of the *Los Angeles Times* stated that *"Toy Story 2* may not have the most original title, but everything else about it is, well, mint in the box." *Chicago Sun Times* critic Roger Ebert, who gave the movie three-and-a half stars out of four, said in his print review, "I forgot something about toys a long time ago, and *Toy Story 2* reminded me." Similarly, *Newsweek*'s David Ansen remarked that "sequels, by definition, are shamelessly commercial enterprises, but when the level of invention is this high you can only be grateful to John Lasseter and his gifted company for giving it their creative all."

John did not take his latest success in stride. If anything, he kept things in perspective. Despite the film's hoopla, he felt that what gave *Toy Story 2* "legs," as he called it, was its heart. "These characters have touched people deeply. They care," he told a reporter. "They relate to it more, to Buzz Lightyear, a character so honest and so good that he just means well, and then to find out all he believed in was completely wrong and how shattering that was. Woody is such a good person, too.

He is put in a situation that any of us would do the same thing. These characters dearly love each other. They are good friends and family."

In the spring of 2000, as with its predecessor, *Toy Story 2* won top honors that year, including a Golden Globe for "Best Picture–Musical or Comedy" (and another nomination for "Best Original Song") and an Academy Award for "Best Original Song." That November, the latest saga in the successful film franchise also swept the Association International du Film d'Animation (ASIFA) at Hollywood's annual Annie Awards, shutting out the well-liked clay-animated spoof *Chicken Run*, and roundly beating other contenders for best feature, such as Disney's *Fantasia/2000*, DreamWorks SKG's *The Road to El Dorado*, and 20th Century Fox's *Titan A.E.*

Following his consecutive string of box-office successes, John remained committed to producing high-quality, family-oriented entertainment. Meeting that goal seemed attainable in his mind. But given the long hours and many sacrifices it took to fulfill those dreams, including missing precious moments with his wife and five sons, the normally energetic animator decided it was time to recharge and put his family before his work.

7

Restoring the Magic of Disney

In the summer of 2000, after an intense run of working straight since 1991 on Pixar's first three movies, *Toy Story*, *A Bug's Life*, and *Toy Story 2*, John's wife Nancy said to him, "Be careful, one day you're gonna wake up and your boys will be going off to college. You will have missed it."

Taking her suggestion, John took the entire summer off. He bought a motor home and traveled cross-country with the entire family. It was the first time in years he was able to spend such a lengthy period of time with his five sons. It would become, in his words, "the highlight" of his life—all of them together 24/7 for two months on the road—having fun and becoming even closer as a family.

After *Toy Story 2*, John had relinquished his reigns as director, serving instead as executive producer while maintaining creative control over future Pixar productions. His contributions made an immediate impact on the studio's continuing success with its two next releases. Produced at Pixar's brand-new, campus-style 225,000 square-foot headquarters in Emeryville, California, and completed by midyear were the studio's upcoming feature *Monsters, Inc.*, and accompanying short-subject *For the Birds*.

In his new role, John was intricately involved in both productions, working alongside *Monsters, Inc.* codirectors Pete Docter and Lee Unkrich and *For the Birds* director Ralph Eggleston. He candidly offered his ideas in their development. Rather than concern himself with the animation and complexities of the production, he continued his strategy of ensuring that every project maintained the Pixar brand of quality family entertainment—a well-crafted story, and well-executed and believable characterizations—that had become hallmarks of his and Pixar's success. "It's always assumed there's a way to make it better at every stage," commented Docter. "John is great at saying, 'Well, what if you did this extra little gesture?' And suddenly it really sparkles and comes to life."

Back in 1994, John and Docter, Andrew Stanton, and Joe Ranft originally hatched the idea of the animated monster epic, *Monsters, Inc.*, over lunch. Out of their brainstorming session, Docter's original concept revolved around a 30-year-old man confronted by monsters he drew in a book as a child that come back into his life as an adult. After scripting the story in 1996, Docter cowrote a treatment of the story in February 1997 (with the Mike Wazowski character added later after a story review meeting in April 1998). Production finally commenced in 2000. This time the film focused on a fish-out-of-water story of monsters—a large, blue-haired behemoth, James P. "Sulley" Sullivan, and his green, one-eyed assistant, Mike Wazowski—that hide in closets and lurk in dark corners to scare children and who accidentally bring back a young girl to their world inhabited solely by monsters.

Thanks to an engaging story line and sophisticated jokes, standards expected in a Pixar film, *Monsters, Inc.* became a monstrous hit following its theatrical release on November 2, 2000. Enjoying the largest three-day opening in the history of Walt Disney Studios and Pixar, not only did the movie keep intact Pixar's consecutive string of films ranking number-one at the box office, but it also shattered previous Pixar box-office records the weekend it opened, grossing $62.5 million. The film became Pixar's sixth highest grossing movie worldwide with $525.3 million and $255.8 million in ticket sales domestically.

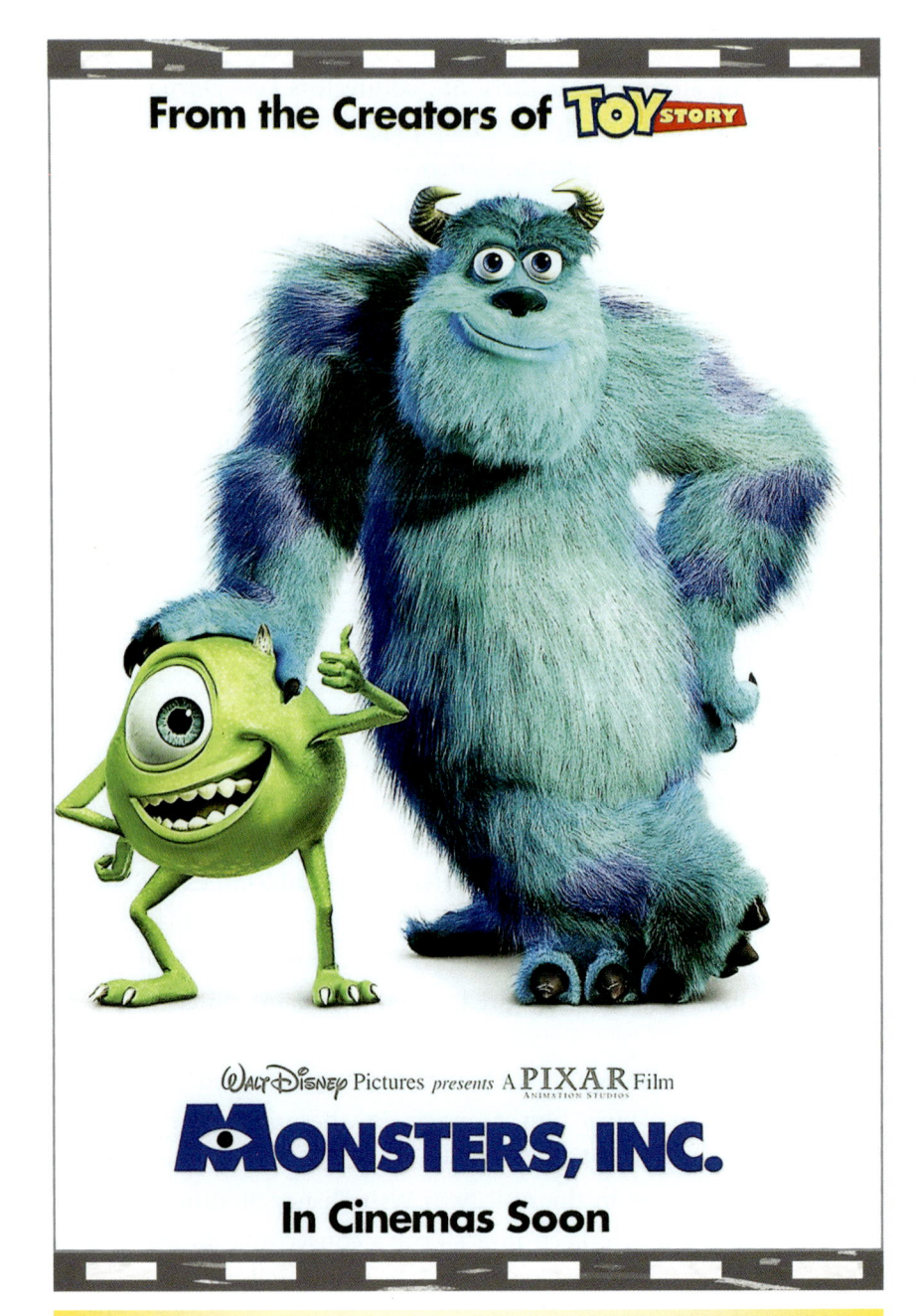

Advance theatrical poster for the blockbuster hit *Monsters, Inc.* (2001), for which Lasseter served as executive producer. *Courtesy: Cinema Poster Archive.* © Disney/Pixar. All rights reserved.

Critics gushed about John's executive producing triumph. The headline to the *Washington Post's* review read, "Monstrously Entertaining," while its critic Desson Howe wrote that *Monsters, Inc.* "is supple and technologically sophisticated entertainment. The characters. . .are veritable kid magnets. Pixar's animation. . .is compelling as ever."

As audiences flocked to movie theaters by droves, members of the Academy of Motion Picture Arts and Sciences recognized the film during that year's annual Academy Awards. *Monsters, Inc.* was nominated for "Best Animation Feature," an honor John shared with the movie's three directors. That June, John was awarded yet another high honor. As part of its regular commencement ceremonies, the American Film Institute's Board of Trustees conferred Honorary Degrees in Fine Arts on him and two others, Lee Grant and Jack Valenti, whose "passion for and commitment to their work is both inspiring and illuminating." In 2001, his producing contribution to Eggleston's clever and entertaining *For the Birds* took first prize at that year's Vancouver Effects and Animation Festival for "Best Animated Computer 3D Short."

For many years John has been an admirer of the work of Japanese animator Hayao Miyazaki, the so-called Walt Disney of Japan. He considers Miyazaki one of his favorite animation directors. In fact, in his L-shaped office brimming with scripts, family pictures, and a multitude of toys at Pixar Animation Studios, John has dedicated one wall as a shrine to his favorite animation director. It includes signed posters, pictures, and mementos from Miyazaki's films. "His films are so specific," John once said. "They have such heart. They're so inventive. They're always inspirational."

Beginning in 2001, John fulfilled his desire of working with the internationally revered animator. He served as executive producer on the American release of Miyazaki's Oscar-winning "Best Animated Feature," *Spirited Away*, and three years later, *Howl's Moving Castle*.

Continuing his role as an executive producer, John and his Pixar team chose their next project wisely. From the world of monsters, they delved to the bottom of the sea producing another fish-out-of-water story, *Finding Nemo*. Written and codirected by Andrew Stanton and Lee Unkrich, the idea for Nemo came to Stanton after seeing a photo of two clown fish peeking out of an anemone. Preproduction of the film began as early as 1997, and production started in January 2000. The film was the last produced using Sun Microsystems computers, and it was dedicated to Pixar animator Glenn McQueen, who died in 2002. The colorful adventure involved a young clown fish, Nemo (Alexander Gould), with one fin smaller than the other that gets captured while his overprotective dad, Marlin (Albert Brooks), along with a regal tang, Dory (Ellen DeGeneres), swim the entire ocean in search of him.

The result was a superb and stunning artistic achievement. Besides breaking weekend box-office records domestically for the opening of an animated feature film, *Finding Nemo* would become Pixar's most profitable feature and highest grossing film of all time, not to mention a cultural phenomenon. Taking in more than $864 million worldwide, the movie earned John and Pixar their second Academy Award for "Best Animated Film." That spring John walked off with a third Academy Award as a producer for his latest computer-animated short featuring the characters from *Monsters, Inc.*, *Mike's New Car*.

The next project John executive produced was truly a super-heroic effort in more ways than one. From scary monsters to sparkling sea, he and Pixar would find magic once more in a story about a family of former masked crime-fighting super-heroes brought out of retirement to battle the world's greatest nemesis—a jilted fan turned evil—in *The Incredibles*. The project reunited John with his former CalArts classmate Brad Bird, who wrote and directed the movie. Originally Bird had developed the idea as a traditional, cel-animated feature for Warner Bros, but after the studio closed down its animated features division, he took it to Pixar.

Remarkably, before the release of *The Incredibles*, under John's supervision and involvement, Pixar's five previous computer-animated features—including *Toy Story*, *Monsters Inc.*, and *Finding Nemo*—had amassed more than $2.5 billion in worldwide box-office revenue and sold more than 150 million DVDs and videos.

The Incredibles became a bona fide hit and won near-universal critical acclaim. Complete with the usual merchandising tie-ins, it elevated

On opposite sides of Lasseter, *Finding Nemo* codirectors Andrew Stanton (left) and Lee Unkrich (right), and producer Graham Walters promote the movie in a unique way in this September 2003 photo. *Courtesy: Le Monde*

profits for the Pixar studio. Opening nationally on November 5, 2004, the breakneck action fantasy film grossed $70.4 million in its opening weekend from 7,600 screens at 3,933 theaters—an average of $17,917 per theater—the highest opening weekend gross for a Pixar film (later broken in 2010 by *Toy Story 3*). Ultimately the movie grossed $261.4 million in the United States and $631.4 million worldwide. It was also honored with numerous awards, including the Academy Award for

"Best Animated Film"—the second for John as producer. As an executive producer, he also walked off with an Oscar for Pixar's latest computer-animated short released that year, *Boundin'*, while the Art Directors Guild honored him with an award for "Outstanding Contribution to Cinematic Imagery." In 2005, John coproduced a computer-animated short that Bird directed featuring the baby Jack-Jack, called *Jack-Jack Attack*, released that March with the DVD version of *The Incredibles*.

Behind the scenes, however, hostility between Pixar founder Steve Jobs and then-Disney chairman Michael Eisner had begun to jeopardize relations between the two companies. Pixar's contract was ready to run out after its next film in production, *Cars*. On January 29, 2004, Jobs surprised Eisner by announcing he was ending negotiations on a new contract. The bickering between the two parties actually predated the latest harangue. After *Toy Story 2* opened in November 1999, a feud broke out between Jobs and Eisner about how Pixar should be run and on what terms Disney would be part of it. At the time, their previous deal was about to expire after Pixar's seventh feature.

Worsening the situation was Eisner's decision to launch a new upstart studio, Circle 7, to franchise Pixar's cartoon stars without them. Disney was in its right as they controlled the rights to all Pixar characters, including those in the upcoming *Cars*. That included producing sequels, made-for-video spin-offs, and theme-park rides based on them. After the breakdown in negotiations Eisner began to staff his surrogate-Pixar computer-animation studio in earnest, eventually filling its roster to around 1,780 artists, writers, executives, and directors.

Asked about Circle 7 during an early April 2004 interview, John would not comment. Privately, however, he was deeply opposed to the idea. *Finding Nemo* writer-director Andrew Stanton called Disney's move "the most expensive bargaining chip ever created."

Pouring millions into the new venture, Disney further angered John and principals of Pixar with its decision to begin production of a *Toy Story 3* with plans for a fourth and follow-ups in development of *Monsters, Inc.* and *Finding Nemo*. Disney hoped that the threat of making sequels more cheaply would chasten them into accepting more favorable renewal terms. Pixar never blinked.

CHANGING DIRECTION

In October 2005, following a long and often ugly battle to unseat him, Eisner finally exited his post. After Robert Iger replaced Eisner as chief operating officer, relations between Disney and Pixar stated to improve. More pragmatic and well liked than his predecessor, he immediately went to work on hammering out a merger deal with Pixar. John had spent the previous years in frustrating negotiations with Eisner—discussions in private meetings were leaked to the public while he was forced to wait months for a counterproposal. But with Iger, negotiations went much smoother. John received a deal that assured total creative control—a more important criterion than money—and allowed Pixar's independence.

On May 5, 2006, the deal closed. Disney purchased Pixar in a deal worth $7.4 billion in Disney stock. Jobs became Disney's biggest individual stockholder and John was appointed chief creative officer of both Pixar and Disney animation studios at an annual salary of $2.5 million through 2011, making him one of the most powerful executives at the studio that had unceremoniously dumped him 23 years earlier. He was also named principal creative advisor at Walt Disney Imagineering to help design attractions for Disney's theme parks. Pixar President Ed Catmull, another of Pixar's chief creative architects, joined John in running all of Disney animation. Under this new arrangement, John reported directly to Iger, bypassing Disney's studio and theme parks executives. He also received greenlight power on films with the consent of Walt Disney's nephew, Roy E. Disney.

Less than 24 hours after the merger was announced at Disney studios in Burbank, John wasted no time asserting his authority by stopping production of the controversial sequel, *Toy Story 3*. One of his immediate tasks was to restore the heritage that had been lost at Walt's cartoon factory. As he told a reporter, "I wanted to celebrate the heritage of this place, because we were kind of creating our own heritage at Pixar. It's great, but coming back here—this is the same studio that Walt Disney started. It's never closed its doors. It's the same studio! And that's what's amazing."

John wanted animators to feel a sense of being part of something much bigger, and he worked hard to create that kind of atmosphere throughout. He also wanted the studio to be led more by filmmakers than executives, a place where movie ideas were not market-strategy driven and where directors could think more about the audience than worry about addressing how executives wanted the films made. John started with changing the name of the studio's animated features division. Called Disney Feature Animation, he went, "No, no, no, no. This is The Walt Disney Animation Studio. That's how everybody on the outside thinks of it, and that's what we are."

In addition to creating a sense of awe and nostalgia internally, John wanted to infuse the timeless values that had made Disney animated movies classic—messages of loyalty, self-sacrifice, and friendship—values that had made his movies at Pixar so transcendent but with a moral compass that made them memorable. "We want these films to be at the same level of the films Walt Disney made," he remarked. "I mean look, he made *Snow White*, *Pinocchio*, *Fantasia*, *Dumbo*, *Bambi*, *Peter Pan*. Those films, they live forever. They will always live forever."

Splitting his time between Disney studios in Burbank and Glendale and the Pixar Animation Studios in Emeryville, John was typically hands-on in his dual role. He attended meetings on movies in development and those in progress, Imagineering projects for Disney theme parks, and products for merchandising and licensing. This was in addition to consulting on other creative activities throughout the company. John was used to juggling between the artist and executive. "Working at Pixar is like being a trapeze artist," he joked, "where you're looking across at the other guy to catch you. Like all great circus artists, you want to do something no one has ever done before."

In the months leading up to the merger, John had waiting in the wings Pixar's final computer-animated feature before it was bought by Disney, *Cars*. The film had put him back at the helm as codirector with Joe Ranft. The movie perfectly blended two of his greatest passions: computer animation and car racing. An avid NASCAR fan, John frequently would attend races at Infineon Raceway near his home in Sonoma, California. He also owned his own race club, JL's Race Club, next to White Gold Club. Originally set to be released on November 4, 2005, *Cars* release date was changed to June 9, 2006. Jobs announced

Lasseter toys around with toy-scale models of race car Lighting McQueen and Mater the tow truck, stars of the first film he directed since *Toy Story 2*, the rollicking family adventure *Cars* (2006). © *Walt Disney Pictures. All rights reserved.*

the date with plans to put all Pixar films on a summer release schedule to allow for holiday sales of their films on DVD. It marked Ranft's final film. He died in a car crash in 2005.

Cars originated from a 1998 original script called *The Yellow Car*. Pixar originally planned to produce it as its next movie after John's *A Bug's Life* for release in early 1999. They scrapped the project, producing *Toy Story 2* instead. Production resumed after the script was overhauled. The idea for *Cars* was born from John's cross-country motor home trip in the summer of 2000. Upon his return, he enlisted the services of Route 66 historian Michael Wallis to lead 11 Pixar animators in rented white Cadillacs on two trips across the famed historical route as research for the film. In 2001, John retitled the movie *Route 66*. But in 2002, to avoid confusion with the 1960 television series of the same name, he changed it to *Cars*.

Released in the summer of 2006, *Cars* is a rollicking adventure about a cocky would-be champion stock car racer, Lightning McQueen (voiced by Owen Wilson), who takes an unanticipated detour to a sleepy Route 66 town and finds what has been missing in his high-octane life. An amazing spectacle of beauty, artistry, and creativity in motion, the movie delivered as expected, producing a tidal wave of acclaim and widespread box-office success.

Before and after the success of *Cars*, John's immense contributions to furthering the art of animation were recognized in great measure. On February 17, 2006, John was awarded the prestigious George Méliès Award for Artistic Excellence by the Visual Effects Society. A month later he was recognized by the exhibition community at its annual ShoWest convention with their first-ever Pioneer of Animation Award. Then, in 2007, John won an Oscar nomination for "Best Animated Film" and garnered a BAFTA nomination for "Best Animated Feature" Film, an Annie nomination for "Best Directing in an Animated Feature Production," and a Hollywood Film Festival award for "Animation of the Year." John was also nominated for an Oscar for "Best Animated Short Film" for *One Man Band*, which he coproduced. The short premiered at the 29th Annecy International Animated Film Festival in France on January 31, 2005, before being jointly released to theaters in the United States with *Cars*.

For release that November with the DVD edition of *Cars,* John codirected, with Dan Scanlon, Pixar's first *Cars Toon*, featuring the broken-down tow-truck Mater and Lighting McQueen, *Mater and the Ghostlight*. Then, that December, he announced Disney's plans to start producing animated shorts in 2-D, CGI, or a combination of both once again for theatrical release. He pushed this plan forward because he deemed the idea of producing shorts an ideal way to train and discover new talent and become a testing ground for new techniques and ideas.

RETURNING TO PRODUCING

After that, John went back to producing. In 2007, he worked behind the scenes on two features, Walt Disney's *Meet the Robinsons*, released on March 30, and helmed by Stephen J. Anderson, and Pixar's *Ratatouille*, Brad Bird's second stint at director that opened in theaters on June 29. *Ratatouille* opened with *Lifted*, a computer-animated short John co-executive produced and that his longtime sound editor, seven-time Academy Award-winner Gary Rydstrom, directed. He also coproduced the first theatrical Goofy solo cartoon short in 46 years, *How to Hook Up Your Home Theater*, codirected by Kevin Deters and Stevie Wermers-Skeleton for Walt Disney Pictures. That year he also coproduced Pixar's first cartoon short featuring traditional animation, *Your Friend the Rat*, for release that November with the DVD edition of *Ratatouille*.

The following year, as executive producer, John also was a key player behind two other features: the Andrew Stanton-directed *WALL•E*, released on June 27 and hailed by critics as a masterpiece, and *BOLT*, which debuted on November 21 in theaters nationwide. Likewise, he executive produced *Presto*, the Academy Award-nominated short shown in theaters with *WALL•E*, and which paid tribute to classic *Looney Tunes* and *Tom and Jerry* cartoons. John served as executive producer on a new computer-animated short as well that was directed by Chuck Williams, *Glago's Guest*. Premiering that June at the Annecy International Animated Film Festival, the film was originally intended to precede *BOLT* in its theatrical release but did not test well with audiences and the Pixar short that John directed, *Tokyo Mater*, was released in its place. In September 2008, John helped executive produce for DisneyToon Studios the first digitally animated direct-to-DVD feature, *Tinker Bell*, the story of Walt Disney's famous flying fairy, set in Pixie Hollow. It was also the first of five features made exclusively for the DVD market. Then, in conjunction with November's DVD releases of *WALL•E*, he coproduced a computer-animated short based on and named after the character from the latter *BURN•E*.

In the case of *BOLT*, Chris Sanders, best known for directing the Disney film *Lilo & Stitch*, was originally contracted to direct it. He had conceived the project for Disney under a different title, *American Dog*. It was already in development when John arrived in 2006. John and his creative team were critical of what they saw and John gave Sanders notes to improve the story, but Sanders resisted. Calling Sanders a "brilliant filmmaker," John felt his vision exceeded what he felt the film should be. So he let him go.

John and Pixar took over the project from Disney and kept Sanders's rough concept. "What really is left is the basic concept that a dog has been raised on the set of a TV show and believes it is real," John explained. Restarting the story as *BOLT*, he brought in two amazing young talents, Chris Williams and Byron Howard, to codirect it. John was by their side through every step of the production. The pair gave the characters and film itself an entirely different look than what Sanders had envisioned and produced the film in a record amount of time. It marked the third time that John changed directors on a project; the first two times were with *Toy Story 2* and *Ratatouille*.

Once again John displayed his mastery of story in making *BOLT* a success. He believed strongly, as he always has, that no amount of good animation can save a weak story. "That's why we'll devote ourselves to reworking the story until it's right," he explained in 2009. "And that's what we did with *BOLT*, working on many of the sequences 20 or 30 times over until we got it just right before we let it go into production. I was adamant that they were not allowed to put something into production until we knew it was working really great."

In the summer of 2009, John attended the world premiere of his latest computer-animated enterprise as a producer, *Up*, featuring the voice of actor Ed Asner (of TV's *The Mary Tyler Moore Show* fame). The film was accompanied in its release by the Pixar animated short directed by Peter Sohn that John also executive produced, *Partly Cloudy*.

Audiences loved *Up*, a film about a lonely, curmudgeonly widower, Carl Fredericksen (Ed Asner), who fulfills the trip of a lifetime to see the wilds of South America by tying thousands of balloons to his home, and who is joined by an eight-year-old stowaway, Russell. The computer-animated adventure made more than $415 million worldwide and won two Oscars at the 82nd Academy Awards, for "Best Animated Feature" and "Academy Award for Best Original Score," as well as two Golden Globes for "Best Original Score" and "Best Animated Feature Film."

Restoring the Magic of Disney 117

Lasseter and his wife Nancy pose for the camera near Hollywood's El Capitan Theatre on the day of the May 2009 premiere of *Up*, the latest Pixar feature he executive produced. *Courtesy: Agence French-Presse*

Up capped a year in which John flourished on other fronts. On July 24, he took the stage at San Diego's Comic-Con International, the world's largest comic book and popular arts convention, to join Japanese animator Hayao Miyazaki to discuss his work in front of a room full of 6,500 admiring fans. It marked the aging artisan's first appearance at the popular event. Upon hearing he planned to make his rare American visit, John was quoted as saying, "If you come over, I'll be by your side the whole time."

Miyazaki's visit was timed with the North American release that August of his third English-dubbed classic animated feature that John executive produced, *Ponyo*, for Walt Disney Pictures.

Lasseter joins his favorite Japanese animation legend Hayao Miyazaki during his first appearance at Comic-Con International, the world's premier comic book and popular arts convention, in July 2009 in San Diego. *Courtesy: Comic-Con*

That September, John was recognized at the 66th edition of the Venice International Film Festival with its Golden Lion Award for lifetime achievement as "one of the protagonists of the innovation in contemporary animated cinema." First bestowed in 1970 to actor-filmmaker Orson Welles, John's longtime friend George Lucas presented him with the honor to a rousing ovation. The award was presented not only to John but also to his crew of Pixar directors—Brad Bird, Pete Docter, Andrew Stanton, and Lee Unkrich. It marked the first time in festival history that the award honored not just one filmmaker but an entire studio. As John told reporters after being honored, "We really set out to deeply entertain an audience, not just children but adults as well."

In October, John produced, in association with DisneyToon Studios, the successful computer-animated direct-to-DVD sequel *Tinker Bell and the Lost Treasure*, the second in the series, and in November, *Dug's Special Mission*, a Pixar cartoon short expressly for release with the DVD and Blu-Ray editions of *Up*.

Later that month John executive produced the animated family feature *The Princess and the Frog*, inspired in part by E.D. Baker's novel, *The Frog Princess*. Opening in limited release in New York and Los Angeles before going nationwide in December, it was the first 2-D traditionally animated film for Walt Disney Pictures since 2004's *Home on the Range*. The movie was notable as it also featured the studio's first black princess (voiced by Anika Noni Rose). In time for the holidays, John also had a hand in producing the entertaining half-hour Christmas special for Walt Disney Animation Studios that aired on ABC, *Disney's Prep & Landing*.

Meanwhile John was busy developing new projects for the big screen. That June, at the Licensing Exposition in Las Vegas, it was announced that he would return to direct a new animated feature, *Winnie the Pooh*, due in theaters in the spring of 2011. Part of his and Disney's increasing commitment to producing hand-drawn animated movies, John gave up directing the project and instead worked closely with its three codirectors, Steve Anderson, Clark Spencer, and Don Hall. Their goal was to create a production closely matching the original looks of the 1960s films by using watercolors the way original Disney

LEGENDS OF ANIMATION

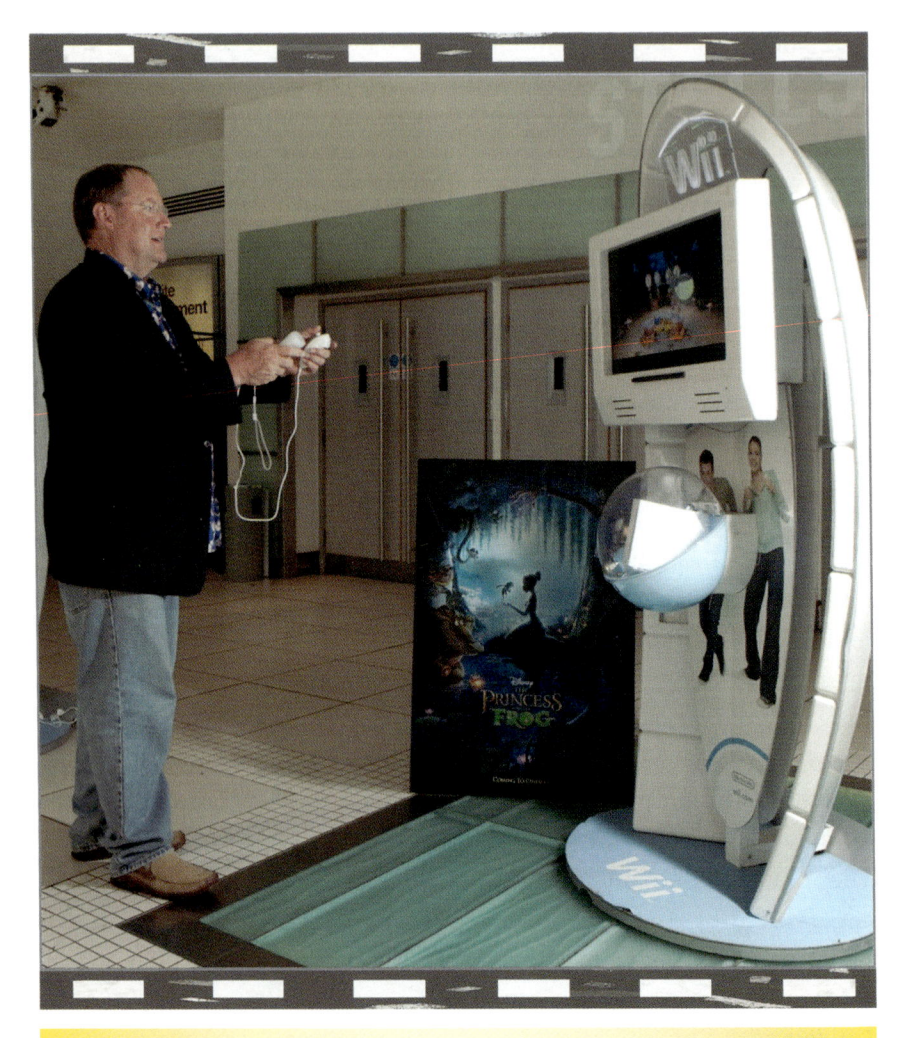

Lasseter tests his skill on the Wii home video game based on Walt Disney Animation Studios' first 2-D traditional, hand-drawn animated feature since 2004, The Princess and Frog.

animators did. As John told the crowd in September 2010, at the second annual D23 Expo, an event that brings the entire world of Disney under one roof at the Anaheim Convention, "Honestly, this is the most blessed production I've ever worked on."

John was also putting the finishing touches on the long-awaited third installment of the *Toy Story* saga, *Toy Story 3*. He had talked about wanting to make another one ever since the second was released. By May 2006, after derailing the Disney-Circle 7-produced sequel, *Toy Story 3* was back in preproduction under Pixar's control. John decided it was time to do the third film and revisit the characters while he and his creative team still had enthusiasm for the characters. He and Andrew Stanton and Pete Docter—two-thirds of the cowriting team of the original 1995 animated film—spent two days brainstorming on ideas in the same little cabin where they wrote the first. Drawing from their life experiences, John tapped into the experience of dropping off his son, Bennett, to go to college at Loyola Marymount University in Los Angeles, as the basis of the story of the second sequel as Woody, Buzz, and the other toys deal with Andy's departure for college. "Driving away, when you leave your child behind at college, all I could think of was him as a little kid, sliding down the slide," John said in a press conference in 2010. "It was very emotional for us."

To get fans pumped up for the third iteration, Disney-Pixar reissued the first two *Toy Story* films to theaters in the spring of 2010, this time in 3-D, with John overseeing the process. While directing the first two, he turned the third film over to Lee Unkrich to helm. Instead John co-executive produced the film and cowrote the story with Oscar-winning screenwriter Michael Arndt (*Little Miss Sunshine*).

Opening in theaters on June 18, 2010, to universal acclaim, *Toy Story 3* preserved John's record of producing hit movies. It broke the record of *Shrek the Third* for the biggest single-day box-office gross in North America of $110.3 million and the highest opening weekend for a Pixar film. On August 27, 2010, the computer-animated fantasy-adventure set a new high, crossing the $1 billion mark, grossing more than $404.9 million domestically and $592.9 million internationally, and becoming Pixar's highest grossing film ever.

As *Toy Story 3* trounced the competition, John was already at work on another feature in an executive producing role for Walt Disney Pictures, *Tangled*. Based on the Brothers Grimm's classic German fairy tale "Rapunzel" (also the project's original working title), the film, featuring the voices of Mandy Moore and Zachary Levi, became the third traditionally hand-drawn feature and 50th in the Walt Disney Animated Classics series. It was released at Thanksgiving that year to mixed

Famous filmmaker and longtime friend George Lucas presents Lasseter with the Golden Lion lifetime achievement award at the Venice International Film Festival. © *Associated Press*

reviews. However, the 100-minute family film, made at a cost of $260 million, took in more than $200.8 million domestically and $590.7 million worldwide.

The same month *Toy Story 3* was unleashed, after much speculation, word broke than John would also share directorial duties with first-time director Brad Lewis to helm the sequel *Cars 2*. Featuring the original cast of cars from the first film, Lighting McQueen (Owen Wilson) and his pit team and his new pit boss Mater motor around Europe in the "Race of Champions," taking them to five different countries—Tokyo, Germany, Italy, Paris, and London—with Mater becoming mired in case of mistaken identity.

Released on June 24, 2011, the 1-hour and 53-minute movie outperformed projected estimates of $50 million to $55 million in ticket sales, grossing $66.1 million its first weekend—$6 million more than the original. This was despite becoming the first Pixar feature to receive mostly negative reviews.

In his spare time, John continues to cultivate other passions. One of them is as a wine grower. He and Nancy own vineyards in Glen Ellen, California, in Sonoma County, one of Northern California's finest winemaking regions, where they produce and sell their own label of wine, Tague (named after Nancy's maiden name). John still enjoys attending NASCAR races at Infineon Raceway in Sonoma and covets among his prized possessions a steam locomotive—the "Marie E."—originally owned by the late Disney legend Ollie Johnston.

At home, John's living room mantel offers glimpses into the people and achievements of his life—his two Oscars, family snapshots of his parents on one side, and a shot of him and Nancy with Tom Hanks and Tim Allen on the other. Flitting between Pixar's base in Emeryville, outside of San Francisco, and Disney's animation studio in Burbank, his greatest joy still comes from entertaining others. "I do what I do because of Walt Disney—his films and his theme park and his characters and his joy in entertaining," he said. "I believe in the nobility of entertaining people and I take great, great pride that people are willing to give me two or three hours of their busy lives."

John gives the credit—not to the advances in computer animation he pioneered—but to what matters the most overall: giving audiences a good story. "From the beginning," he said, "I kept saying it's not the technology that's going to entertain audiences, it's the story."

From his first film many years ago to his latest, John's instincts have proven him right. For this so-called guru of computer animation, the world remains his stage and is a much better place thanks to his creations, his heart, and his inventiveness. With passion and enthusiasm, he continues to inspire and entertain audiences to the farthest reaches around the world and take animation to new heights.

SELECTED RESOURCES

For further study of John Lasseter's work and career, the following resources are recommended:

Filmography

John Lasseter Filmography (http://www.imdb.com/name/ nm0005124/)

This up-to-date filmography provides titles, credits, release dates, and synopses of every production from Lasseter's career.

DVD and Video Collections

Tiny Toy Stories (Buena Vista Entertainment, 1996)

This video collection of five shorts written, animated, and directed by Lasseter and produced by Pixar between 1984 and 1989, includes *The Adventures of André & Wally B.*, *Luxo Jr.*, *Red's Dream*, the Oscar-winning *Tin Toy*, and *Knick Knack*.

Pixar Short Films Collection, Vol. 1 (Walt Disney Video, 2007)

This single-disc DVD collection offers 13 complete and uncut Pixar computer-animated shorts including Lasseter's, among them *The Adventure of Andre & Wally B.*, *Luxo Jr.*, *Red's Dream*, *Tin Toy*, *Knick Knack*, *Geri's Game*, *For the Birds*, *Mike's New Car*, *Boundin'*, *Jack-Jack Attack*, *Mater and the Ghostlight*, *One Man Band*, and *Lifted*, plus the documentary extra: *The Pixar Shorts: A Short History*.

Disney Pixar Three-Pack (Toy Story/A Bug's Life/Toy Story 2) (Walt Disney Home Video, 1998)

In celebration of Pixar's 15th anniversary, this video set features three of the most beloved computer-animated films ever made, directed by Lasseter, in one collection: *Toy Story*, *A Bug's Life*, and *Toy Story 2*, presented in Dolby Digital sound. Extras include the Oscar-winning shorts *Tin Toy* and *Geri's Game*, and Oscar-nominated short *Luxo Jr.*, plus hilarious outtakes.

The Pixar Story (Walt Disney Home Video, 2008)

This DVD edition of filmmaker Leslie Iwerks's Oscar- and Emmy-nominated 2007 documentary, released exclusively as part of the three-disc special edition of *WALL•E*, traces the creation and history of the groundbreaking company, with conversations with animators, producers, directors, and voices actors, that forever changed Hollywood animation.

SELECTED BIBLIOGRAPHY

Adams, Guy. "John Lasseter: To Infinity and Beyond." *Independent* (U.K.). 17 July 2001. Available online. URL: http://www.independent.co.uk/news/people/profiles/john-lasseter-to-infinity-and-beyond-2028718.html.

Adolphson, Sue. "Malevolent Baby Terrorizes Toys–Oscar-winning *Tin Toy* Featured in 20-piece Festival of Animation." *San Francisco Chronicle*. April 9, 1989.

Avalos, George. "Pixar Picked to Produce 1st Computer-Generated Movie." *Contra Costa Times*. July 13, 1995.

Baltake, Joe. "Computoons a Byte of This, a Byte of that in a Video Art Smorgasbord That Only Whets the Appetite." *Sacramento Bee*. April 1, 1988.

Block, Alex Ben. "Animator John Lasseter Making Disney a Top Draw." *Reuters*. October 23, 2008. Available online. URL: http://www.reuters.com/article/idUSTRE49M3E620081023?pageNumber=1.

Booth, Cathy. "The Wizard of Pixar." *Time*. December 14, 1998.

Brown, Corie. "Movies—Ants in Their Pants—DreamWorks and Pixar Anxiously Await the War of the Insect Movies." *Newsweek*. September 28, 1998. Corliss, Richard. "Review: *Toy Story*." *Time*. November 27, 1995.

———. "All Too Superhuman." *Time*. October 25, 2004.

Daly, Steve. "The Man Who Could Save Animation." *Entertainment Weekly*. April 21, 2006. Available online. URL: http://www.ew.com/ew/article/0,,1186017,00.html.

"Disney Joins Computer Age." *Daily News* (Los Angeles, CA). July 13, 1991.

Fitchko, T.R. "Future of Art Drawn–Computer-Made Animation Topic of Festival Opener." *Columbus Dispatch*. October 27, 1989.

Fleeman, Michael. "Of Ants, Bugs and Rug Rats: The Story of Dueling Bug Movies." *Associated Press*. September 23, 1998.

Frost, John. "John Lasseter Talks About *BOLT*." *The Disney Blog*. March 24, 2009. Available online. URL: http://thedisneyblog.com/2009/03/24/john-lasseter-talks-about-bolt/.

Gant, Charles. "Talk of the Toon: Pixar." *Times* (London, England). 8 November 2003.

Garcia, Chris. "*Toy Story* Impact Surprised Lasseter." *Press Democrat*. March 24, 1996.

Garner, Jack. *USA Today*. April 25, 1988.

Gleiberman, Owen. "Review: *Toy Story*." *Entertainment Weekly*. November 24, 1995.

———. "Review: *A Bug's Life*." *Entertainment Weekly*. November 27, 1998.

Gliatto, Tom. "Review: Toy Story." *People*. November 27, 1995.

———. "Review: *A Bug's Life*." *People*. November 30, 1998.

Guthman, Edward. "Four Marin-Based Animation Wizards Win Oscars." *San Francisco Chronicle*. March 31, 1989.

Hawkins, Robert J. "Disney Animation's Golden Age Returns." *San Diego Union-Tribune*. June 19, 1994.

———. "*Toy Story* Rockets Disney Into Digital Animation Era." *San Diego Union-Tribune*. November 21 1995.

Hershenson, Karen. "Pixar's Toy Boy." *Contra Costa Times*. November 20, 1995.

"Inanimate Objects Emote on Screen." *American Cinematographer*. May 1987.

"Industry Activities: Eight Student Filmmakers from Across the Nation Win Honors in Motion Picture Academy Competition." *American Cinematographer*. July 1980.

"John Lasseter." *Authors and Artists for Young Adults*. Vol. 65. Detroit, Mich.: Thomson Gale, 2005.

Joseph, Greg. "*Tin Toy* Plays with High-Tech Animation." *Evening Tribune* (San Diego, Calif.). March 1, 1989.

Klawans, Stuart. "Review: *A Bug's Life*." *The Nation*. December 21, 1998.

Kreiswirth, Sandra. "Toying with History—Computer Graphics Team Admits High-Tech Nothing Without Story." *Daily Breeze* (Torrance, Calif.). November 24, 1995.

Lally, Kevin. "Catching Nemo." *Film Journal International.* May 2003.

LeBaron, Gaye. "Bicycle Bunni: 'Burbank's Right!'" *Press Democrat.* April 29, 1996.

Lee, Nora. "Computer Animation Comes of Age." *American Cinematographer.* October 1989.

———. "Computer Animation Demystified, Part II." *American Cinematographer.* November 1989.

Levander, Michelle. "Baby Wins an Oscar Award Scores One for Computer Animation." *San Jose Mercury News.* April 1, 1989.

Lasseter, John. "Buzz Lightyear Gets Dirty." *Forbes.* December 1, 1997.

McConahey, Meg. "Computer Animation Maestro Caught Up in Magic of Moment." *Press Democrat.* October, 29, 1995.

———. "Disney Opening in Sonoma *Toy Story* Has Pre-Hollywood Black-Tie Debut." *Press Democrat.* October, 29, 1995.

McCracken, Harry. "Luxo Sr.: An Interview with John Lasseter." *Animato.* Winter 1990.

McNary, Dave. "Animated Agreement—Disney to Co-Produce Five Computer-Generated Movies with Company Involved in *Toy Story*." *Daily News* (Los Angeles, Calif.). February 25, 1997.

Mandell, Paul. "Young Sherlock Holmes: A 'What If' Tale." *American Cinematographer.* March 1986.

Mason, Clark. "Sonoma Sparkles with Glamour as Disney's *Toy Story* Unveiled." *Press Democrat.* November 12, 1995.

"Only Three Locals in the Oscar Race." *San Francisco Chronicle.* February 12, 1987.

McCarthy, Todd. "Review: *A Bug's Life*." *Variety.* November 22, 1999.

Price, David A. *The Pixar Touch.* New York: Alfred A. Knopf, 2008.

"PROFILE: John Lasseter." *The Sunday Times.* October 25, 2009.

Richardson, John H. "The Auteur of Computer Cartoons—Oscar Winner John Lasseter." Technical Artist." *Daily News* (Los Angeles, Calif.). May 27, 1989.

Ross, Jonathan. "John Lasseter." *Guardian Online.* 19 November 2001. Available online.URL: http://www.guardian.co.uk/.

Santa Rita, Michael. "High Tech *Toy* for Director." *Washington Times.* April 25, 1996.

Schickel, Richard. "Review: *Toy Story 2.*" *Time.* November 29, 1999.

Shay, Jody Duncan. "*Young Sherlock Holmes*: Anything But Elementary." *Cinefex.* Issue 26. May 1986.

Sheehan, Henry. "Forget the Hype–It's Just a Buddy Flick." *The Orange County Register.* November 19, 1995.

Sherman-Savage, Maurina. "Festival Again Demonstrates Animation Not Just for Kids." *Evening Tribune* (San Diego, Calif.). February 17, 1990.

Silver, Miriam. "A *Toy Story* Tale—Pixar's Creative Director, a Father of Five Boys, Knows All About Children's Playthings." *Press Democrat.* November 14, 1999.

Sragow, Michael. "Computertoons." *New York Times News Service.* November 12, 1995.

Stack, Peter. "Toying with Animation—Disney's First Entirely Computer-Animated Feature Hits the Big Screen." *San Francisco Chronicle.* November 19, 1995.

———. "Rivalry Doesn't Bug Local Animators—Both New Insect Films Came From Area Studios." *San Francisco Chronicle.* November 5, 1998.

Steffens, Daneet. "Review: Toy Story: The Art and Making of the Animated Film." *Entertainment Weekly.* December 15, 1995.

Strauss, Bob. "*Toy* Looks Like Child's Play, But . . ." *Daily News* (Los Angeles, Calif.). November 19, 1995.

———. "Making a Mountain Out of an Anthill—Pixar Colonizes Computer Graphics with *A Bug's Life*." *Daily News* (Los Angeles, Calif.). November 15, 1998.

Tribby, Mike. "Review: *Toy Story*: The Art and Making of the Animated Film." *Booklist.* November 1, 1995.

Villagran, Nora. "*Luxo Jr.* in Line for Best Animated Short—Who Says the Computer Can't Generate an Oscar?" *San Jose Mercury News.* March 29, 1987.

Whipp, Glenn. "Swimming Against the Tide: Pixar Crew Encourages Limitless Creativity and Interaction at Enormous Bay Area Building." *Daily News.* May 30, 2003.

Yabroff, Jennie. "35: John Lasseter: Pixar's Animation Guru Dominates the Global Box Office, Even in Tough Times." *Newsweek.* December 20, 2008.

INDEX

Page numbers in *italics* indicate photos or illustrations.

A

The Abyss 55
Academy Awards. *See* Awards/nominations
The Adventures of André & Wally B. 35–38
advertising 81
Aladdin 17, 69
Allen, Tim *74*, 74–75, 82–83
Allen, Woody 94
American Film Institute 107
Anderson, Stephen J. 115, 119
Animation Motion 40
Annie Awards 87, 114
Ansen, David 84, 102
Antz 94–96
Arndt, Michael 121
Arnold, Bonnie 70, 72
The Art of Animation (Thomas) 14
ASIFA awards 103
Asner, Ed 116
avars 77
Avery, Tex 64
awards/nominations
 for *Boundin'* 110
 for *Finding Nemo* 108
 for *Geri's Game* 90
 Golden Lion Lifetime Achievement Award 119, *122*
 for *The Incredibles* 109–110
 for *Luxo Jr.* 50–51
 for *Mike's New Car* 108
 for *Monsters, Inc.* 107
 multiple 114
 for *Presto* 115
 for *Red's Dream* 52
 Student Academy 21
 for *Tin Toy* 61–63, *62*
 for *Toy Story* series 85–87, *86*, 103
 for *Up* 116–117
 for *Young Sherlock Holmes* 43

B

babies *53*, 54–63, *57*
BAFTA awards 114
Baker, E.S. 119
Baltake, Joe 50
Barker, Cordell 50
Batman 17
Beauty and the Beast 30
bicycles 47, *48*, 52, 63
Bird, Brad 17, 24, 108, 115, 119
birth of John Lasseter 11
Black Friday 75
Blinn, John 49
Bluth, Don 23

130

Index

BOLT 115–116
Boundin' 110
Brannon, Ash 100
The Brave Little Toaster 30–32, 40
Brooks, Albert 108
Buck, Chris 17
buddy pictures 72
Bugcam 92
A Bug's Life 91–92, 93–97, 100
BURN-E 115
Burton, Tim 17, 24
Burtt, Ben 37

C

California Institute of the Arts (CalArts) 16, 17–22
camera positioning 56
Cameron, James 55
cars, interest in 12
Cars 110, 112–114, *113*
Cars Toon 114
Cars 2 122–123
Catmull, Ed 31–35, 40, 46–49, 69, 90, 111
Christiansen, Eric 42–43
A Christmas Carol 27
Circle 7 110
Clements, Ron 73
Cocoon II 58
collaboration 18, 35, 44, 66
Colossal Pictures 69
Comic-Con conventions *118*, 118
commercials 69
Computer Animation Production System (CAPS) 69
computer errors 78
Computer Graphics Division (Lucasfilm) 31, 33–35, 40
computers 37, 39, 55, 108
computer time 78
Condie, Bill 50
controversy 92–95
Cook, Dick 71
Corliss, Richard 84, 97

D

Davis, Marc 24
Debney, John 30
Decker, Spike 60
DeGeneres, Ellen 108
Dennis the Menace (Ketchum) 13
Deters, Kevin 115
dialogue 20–21, 67
Digital Effects 28
Diller, Phyllis 96
Disch, Thomas 30
Disney, Roy E. 111
Disney, Walt 16, 24–25, 39
Disney Animation Studio 112
Disneyland 18–20
Disney's Prep & Landing 119
Disney Studios 13–14, 23–32, 60, 89–90, 92–96, 110–112
DisneyToon Studios 119
Docter, Pete 71–72, 99, 100, 105, 119, 121
DreamWorks Animation 89, 94–96
Driessen, Paul 50
Dug's Special Mission 119
Dumbo 13–14, 18

E

Ebert, Roger 102
education 14, 16–22
Eggleston, Ralph 105
Eisner, Michael 68–70, 89, 110–111
expressions, facial 56

F

Festival of Animation 60
Finding Nemo 64, 107–108, *109*, 110
firing by Disney 32
Fitzpatrick, Bob 23
Foley, Dave 96
For the Birds 104–105, 107
The Fox and the Hound 27–28
freelancing 33, 34
The Frog, the Dog, and the Devil 51

G

George Méliès Award for Artistic Excellence 114
Geri's Game 90
Giles, Corie Brown 97
Glago's Guest 115
Gleiberman, Owen 84, 97
Gliatto, Tom 97
Golden Globes 85, 103, 116
Golden Lion Lifetime Achievement Award 119, *122*
Golden Nica Award 61
go-motion system 41
Good, Craig 56
Gould, Alexander 108
Grant, Lee 107
A Greek Tragedy 51
Gregory, Andre 35
Gribble, Mike 60
Guggenheim, Ralph 66, 72, 76

H

Hall, Don 119
Hanks, Tom 74–75, 82–83
Hannah, Jack 16–17
Hansen, Ed 14, 31–32
Haskett, Dan 24
Hawaiian shirts 66
Hee, Thornton "T." 17, 21
Hercules 17, 96
Howard, Byron 116
Howe, Desson 107
Howl's Moving Castle 107
How to Hook Up Your Home Theater 115

I

Ice Age 29
Iger, Robert 111
The Illusion of Life (Thomas and Johnston) 24
The Incredibles 17, 108–110
Industrial Light & Magic 31, 41–44, 87

International Animated Film Society 87
International Animation Festival 59, 63
The Iron Giant 17
Iwerks, Ub 25

J

Jack-Jack Attack 110
Jacobsen, Nina 95
Jobs, Steve 45, 68–70, 81, 84, 89–90, 110, 111
Johnson, Tim 95
Johnston, Ollie 17, 24, 39, 52
Jones, Chuck 13, 39, 64
Joyce, William 73
Jungle Cruise 20
Jurassic Park 55

K

Kahl, Milt 39–40
Katzenberg, Jeffrey 68–71, 73, 75, 94–96
Keane, Glen 16–17, 24, 26–27, 29–31
Kempley, Rita 84
Ketchum, Hank 13
Kimball, Ward 39
Klawans, Stuart 97
Knick Knack 47, 64–65, *65*
Kroyer, Bill 24, 28
Kunde's Wine Waves party 85–87

L

Lady and the Lamp 20–21
lamps 20–21, 46–51, 58, 63
Larson, Eric 17, 24
Lasseter, Bennett (son) 63
Lasseter, Jackson (son) 63
Lasseter, Jewell (mother) 12, 14
Lasseter, Jim (brother) 11, 12
Lasseter, Joey (son) 52, 80
Lasseter, Johanna (sister) 11, 12

Lasseter, Nancy (wife) 52–54, 80, 82–83, 101, 104, 123
Lasseter, Paul (father) 11–12
Lasseter, P.J. (son) 63
Lasseter, Sam (son) 63
layoffs 70
Leffler, Sam 46
Levinson, Barry 41
Levinthal, Adam 39
Levy, Lawrence 90
Lewis, Brad 122
licensing 55, 87
lighting 51–52
The Lion King 69
Listerine bottles 69
The Little Mermaid 17, 69
logos 50
Louis-Dreyfus, Julia 96
Lucas, George 31, 39, 45, 119, *122*
Lucasfilm Computer Graphics Division 31, 33–35, 40
Luxo Jr. 46–51, 58, 63

M

MAGI/Synthavision 28
Malle, Louis 35
Mann, Jeff 42–43
mascots 50
Maslin, Janet 102
Mater and the Ghostlight 114
Mayer, Mercer 21
McCarthy, Tom 97
McDonald, Timmy 54
McDowall, Roddy 96
McEntee, Brian 30
McFerrin, Bobby 64
McLaren, Norman 40
McQueen, Glenn 108
Meet the Robinsons 115
mergers 111–112
Mickey's Christmas Carol 28
Mike's New Car 108
Miller, Ron 23, 31–32
Miyazaki, Hayao 107, 118, *118*

Monsters, Inc. 104–107, *106*, 110
Moore, Bill 17
motion blur 37
motor home vacation 104, 114
multiplane cameras 28
Muren, Dennis 41, 43–44, 87
music scores 64, 76, 85
Musker, John 17, 24, 73
My Breakfast with André 35

N

NASCAR 112, 123
Newman, Randy 76
"Nine Old Men" 17, 24
Nitemare 21

O

O'Connor, Kendall 17
Oilspot and Lipstick 69
One Hundred and One Dalmatians 25, 26
One Man Band 114
Ostby, Eben 46–47, 52, 61

P

Paik, Karen 99
Partly Cloudy 116
Peanuts (Schulz) 13
Pencil Test 54, 59
Pepperdine University 17
Peterson, Bob 90
Ph.Ds 35, 56
PhotoRealistic RenderMan 55
Pierce, David Hyde 96
Pinkava, Jan 90
Pink Panther movies 27
Pioneer of Animation Award 114
Pixar Animation Studios 45–46, 68–71, 83–84, 89–90, 110–112
Pixar Computer Group 45
Pixar Image Computer 39, 45, 52
Plummer, Elmer 17
Pocahontas 78

Ponyo 118
Porter, Tom 39, 46
Potts, Annie 83
Presto 115
Price, David 95
The Prince of Egypt 96
The Princess and the Frog 119, *120*
Prix Ars Electronica 61
procedural animation 47
Project Athena 37
puppets 41

R

Raiders of the Lost Ark 37
Ranft, Joe 30, 71, 100, 105, 112–113
Ratatouille 115, 116
Ratzenberger, John 83
Red's Dream 47, 48, 52, 63
Rees, Jerry 24, 28
Reeves, Julia 54
Reeves, William
  The Adventures of André & Wally B. and 35–36
  Luxo Jr. and 46–47, 51
  Tin Toy and 61, *62*
  A Tin Toy's Christmas and 69
  Young Sherlock Holmes and *38*, 41
Reitherman, Woolie 24
RenderMan 31, 68, 70
repetitive stress injuries 101
The Return of Jafar 99
REYES (Renders Everything You Ever Saw) technology 31
Richardson, John H. 50
Rickles, Don 83
RM-1 computer 55
Rose, Anika Noni 119
Rotoscoping 41
Route 66 114
Rydstrom, Gary 47–49, 58, 87, 115

S

Sanders, Chris 115–116

San Francisco International Film Festival 63
Scanlon, Don 114
Schneider, Peter 75
Schulz, Charles 13
Schumacher, Thomas 70, 75, 77, 94
scores 64, 76, 85
The Sea Wolf 82
Selick, Henry 24
Sendak, Maurice 29
sequels 99. *See also Toy Story 2*
Shawn, Wallace 35, 83
SIGGRAPH conventions 39, 46, 49, 52, 59
Silver Berlin Bear 52
Smith, Alvy Ray 31, 33, 35, 46, 69
snowman 47, 64–65, *65*
Snow White and the Seven Dwarfs 24–25
Sohn, Peter 116
Sonoma Valley Education Foundation 96
sound effects 37, 47–48, 58
Spacey, Kevin 96
Speed 71
Spencer, Clark 119
Spielberg, Steven 41, 55, 94–95
Spirited Away 107
Sprocket Systems 47
squash-and-stretch style animation 37
Stained Glass Knight Character *38*, 41–44, *42*
Stanton, Andrew
  on Circle 7 110
  Finding Nemo and 107–108, *109*
  Golden Lion Lifetime Achievement Award and 119
  Monsters, Inc. and 105
  Pencil Test and 54
  Toy Story series and 71–72, 100, 121
  WALL-E and 115
Star Trek II:: The Wrath of Khan 40
Star Wars 18, 31, 37, 40
Stock, Rodney 39

Student Academy Awards 21
supercomputers 37
Susman, Galyn 54
The Sword in the Stone 14

T

Tague, Nancy A. *See* Lasseter, Nancy (wife)
Tague wine label 123
Tangled 121
Tarzan 17
Terminator 2: Judgment Day 55
texture mapping 63
texture mattes 43
There's a Nightmare in My Closet (Mayer) 21
Thomas, Bob 14
Thomas, Frank 17, 24, 30, 39, 52
3-D animation 64
timing, importance of 20
Tinker Bell 115, 119
Tin Toy 53, 54–63, *57*
A Tin Toy's Christmas 69
Tiny Toy Stories 87
Tokyo Mater 115
toy collection 25, 66, 99
Toy Story
　first version of 71–75
　initial idea for 70
　revised version of 75–81, *79*
　success of 81–88, *86*
Toy Story 2 98, 99–103, 110
Toy Story 3 110, 111, 120–123
III (Triple-I) 28
TRON 28, 29, 30
Tropicana Orange Juice 69
Turan, Kenneth 102
tuxedos 51, 85

U

Unkrich, Lee 100, 105, 107–108, *109*, 119, 121
Up 116–118, *117*

V

Valenti, Jack 107
Vancouver Effects and Animation Festival 107
Venice International Film Festival 119
Verney, Jim 83
vineyards 123

W

Wall-E 115
Wallis, Michael 114
Walt Disney Animation Studio 112
Walt Disney Feature Animation 68–73
Walt Disney Imagineering 111
Walt Disney Studios 13–14, 23–32, 60, 89–90, 92–96, 110–112
Walters, Graham *109*
Waterworld 71
Wedge, Chris 29
Welles, Orson 119
Wermers-Skelton, Stevie 115
Whedon, Joss 71–72
Where the Wild Things Are (Sendack) 29
Whittier High School 14
Who Framed Roger Rabbit 59, 63
Wild Things test film 29–31
Wilhite, Tom 29, 30, 31, 40
Williams, Chris 116
Williams, Chuck 115
Williams, Richard 27
Willie Wonka & the Chocolate Factory 53
Wilson, Owen 114, 122
Winnie the Pooh 119–120

Y

Young Sherlock Holmes 38, 41–44, *42*
Your Friend the Rat 115

ABOUT THE AUTHOR

Photo courtesy: Brian Maurer.

Jeff Lenburg is an award-winning author, celebrity biographer, and nationally acknowledged expert on animated cartoons who has spent nearly three decades researching and writing about this lively art. He has written nearly 30 books—including such acclaimed histories of animation as *Who's Who in Animated Cartoons*, *The Great Cartoon Directors*, and four previous encyclopedias of animated cartoons. His books have been nominated for several awards, including the American Library Association's "Best Non-Fiction Award" and the Evangelical Christian Publishers Association's Gold Medallion Award for "Best Autobiography/Biography." He lives in Arizona.